With warmest best
wishes to Mr. Bill Kelly.

Most sincerely,
Mrs. Frank Roger Seaver

April 16, 1980

# THE LEGACY OF
# FRANK ROGER SEAVER

Bill Youngs

PEPPERDINE UNIVERSITY PRESS

Frank Roger Seaver

To the Present and Future Students

of

Seaver College

on

This Sixtieth Anniversary of the Marriage

of

Frank and Blanche Seaver

September 16, 1976

# Table of Contents

Frank Roger and Blanche Ebert Seaver

# Preface

This is the story of the man whose life made possible the establishment of Seaver College of Pepperdine University. That a new college should have emerged from the legacy of Frank R. Seaver seems, in retrospect, almost inevitable. The story portrays a consistent, strong man, with determined purpose and will and faith, who was also capable of deep compassion and guileless loyalties.

Equally important, it reveals the strength of Blanche Seaver, the woman who stood beside him for half a century and then committed her individual energies to a single purpose — carrying out the terms of the legacy as she believed Frank intended. As a love story, *The Legacy of Frank Roger Seaver* traces the love the Seavers had not only for each other, but for their fellowman. It is a testimony to their love for a nation whose legacy of freedom gave them the opportunity to create so great a legacy of their own.

Finally, this is a story of faith. Here was a young man who, because he set definite goals from which his eyes never wavered, because he saved and labored long and insistently demanded the same of those in his employ, built a great industrial empire. Here was a gifted young woman who sacrificed her own promising career in music to become a gracious and inspiring helpmeet and thus created one of the most powerful partnerships in American history.

If this book captures the character of Frank Roger Seaver, the credit belongs to those who told me the story. The assessment of his friends, whom I interviewed over many months and in many places, revealed a remarkable consistency. Dr. James W. Fifield, Jr., who as his minister may have known him best, summed up their characterizations in one word — "constant." To relate the birth of Mr. Seaver in San Jose with the happenings of his time, my research took me to the old newspaper stacks of Stanford University. Similar searches were pursued in the Los Angeles library and at Pomona College. One memorable day was spent driving and hiking the canyons, hills and streams near Pomona where young Frank Seaver and his fellow "Knights of the Dagger" spent adventuresome weekend outings. Alone in those quiet hills that day, I felt I really began to know this man whom I had only met once prior to his death in 1964.

I am indebted to Jan Werner Watson's *The Story of the Seavers*, published in 1960 by Pomona College, and to professors at Pomona College, boyhood friends, business associates, and employees of the Hydril Company.

I am also indebted to Dr. James R. Wilburn who invested many hours in fine tuning and editing the final manuscript and supervising publication details.

Although I sifted through volumes of scrapbooks and yellowed and aged newspaper clippings and photographs, the more intimate details came directly from the members of the family. Frank Seaver's nephew, Richard C. Seaver of Los Angeles, and Mrs. Seaver's nephews Earl and Ted Spencer of San Francisco, supplied penetrating insights, as did Mrs. Seaver's sister, Mable Marks, the mother of Ted and Earl. All of them remember him in fulfillment of the Bible verse: "Be ye steadfast, unmovable, always abounding in the work of the Lord" (I Cor. 15:58). Above all, this story came from Mr. Seaver's beloved Blanche and, in a profound sense, it is *her* story as well.

Interestingly, the best interviews I had with Mrs. Seaver were in airplanes flying to and from her sister's home in San Mateo. In the Seaver house at 20 Chester Place, so rich with memories, Mrs. Seaver found it difficult to stay with the subject at hand. In her home she is a literal dynamo of activity, attending to her amazing schedule of interests and commitments. But in an airplane she became a different person — one who, removed from the demands of telephone and visitors and secretaries and pressing duties, recalled so very vividly the fifty years she shared with her beloved Frank. Her hope, and mine, was that those who read the results might be able to share in the inspiration and in the legacy.

So, together up there in the skies, we did our best to get it down on paper.

—Bill Youngs
Pepperdine University
June 1976

# 1

## The Birth of a College

Brilliant Malibu sunshine bathed the crowd and the amphitheater, snuggly set in the heart of the 623 acre campus which slopes, first precipitously, then gently from towering mountains to the blue Pacific.

Dr. William Stivers, long-time university professor, touched the keys of the organ at the top of the bowl of redwood benches and the strains of the "Triumphal March" began.

The principals in the solemn procession, clad in flowing academic regalia, walked slowly down the west stairs and made their way to the platform in front of the chapel.

A college student, Ralph Beck, led the audience in the National Anthem, and Fritz Huntsinger, Sr., facing the audience and the huge academic complex that bears the Huntsinger name, led the Pledge of Allegiance. Dr. Warren Kilday, another member of the faculty, gave the invocation.

The date was April 20, 1975. The scene was the new Malibu campus of Pepperdine University. And 3300 — some standing, others seated — had gathered to officially dedicate Frank R. Seaver College as the first college of the university to be so dedicated.

Frank Seaver would have liked the way Fritz Huntsinger, his contemporary in the oil tool industry, handled the Pledge of Allegiance. It was not sufficient simply for Fritz to put his hand over his heart and mutter the familiar phrases. He first told what the words really meant to him as a young German immigrant to America at about the same time Frank Seaver was beginning his own life's work. Frank Seaver would have joined the ovation which the audience gave to this moving scene before the American flag.

On the platform, Blanche Seaver smiled her own appreciation.

As Fritz Huntsinger and the audience sat down, Richard C. Seaver, nephew of the man being honored and his successor as president of the great Hydril Company, came to the microphone to introduce California Governor, Ronald Reagan. Frank Seaver would also have applauded what his friend Ronald Reagan had to say about independent education. It had groomed Frank well for his amazing career and he had supported it devotedly and generously, both in his own lifetime and through the legacy he left with Blanche.

Reagan called for the preservation of traditional, independent schools and colleges at all costs as "our greatest guarantee of academic freedom." He continued, "In a world that seems to be in so much turmoil, when old and valued traditions are being challenged, there is special joy in seeing this new college come into being — a place where the values that have been tested by time will be passed along to generations yet unborn."

Then the Governor turned his thoughts to those responsible for the new college in Malibu. He spoke of his great respect and admiration for the life and influence of both Blanche and Frank Seaver.

Midway through the dedication ceremony, the Pepperdine A Capella Chorus sang several selections. Appropriately, among them was Blanche Seaver's own moving composition, "Just for Today," a prayer.

Then, university president, Dr. William S. Banowsky, came to the rostrum to deliver the dedicatory address, "A Spirit of Purpose." His comments were reminiscent of his earlier speech, "A Spirit of Place," delivered five years before on these same hills before the hilltops were smoothed and the valley filled to prepare for the beautiful buildings which now graced the scene. As he recalled the dream of George and Helen Pepperdine, Mrs. Pepperdine, widow of the founder, was there to listen and participate further in the making of history.

Almost forty years earlier, the Pepperdines had established a small college on a thirty-three acre campus at the edge of Los Angeles. Now the Pepperdine dream had grown into a multi-campus university enrolling almost 8,000 students in several colleges and professional schools. Coming years would doubtless witness the formal dedication of other academic components which, taken together, would comprise the University. The several parts would be a unified whole under the Pepperdine banner, each reflecting in its own best way, the Pepperdine philosophy of Christian education.

The new Malibu college was to be the central core of the whole academic enterprise. By April 20, 1975, the classic undergraduate college of letters, arts and science around which the professional and graduate schools of the University were to be clustered, had already been set as the cornerstone.

"From this day forward," Dr. Banowsky noted, "it shall be known as the Frank R. Seaver College."

Seaver College had been planned to remain small. With a maximum enrollment of 1800, its academic integrity and special identity would be fiercely guarded. It continues to feature close personal relationships between its students and a faculty whose men and women are of the highest academic training. Combined with academic excellence, young people enrolled in Seaver College have already developed a reputation for the highest standards of personal conduct. On a campus which the *Los Angeles Times* called "one of the most beautiful in the world," Seaver College is purposely designed to make a lasting impact upon the minds and hearts of students.

George Pepperdine, who launched the dream, and Frank R. Seaver, who gave it dramatic acceleration, were contemporaries. They were acquainted during the time Mr. Pepperdine was expanding his Western Auto Supply Stores and Mr. Seaver was creating his great Hydril Company. Rugged individualists, inventive, long-range thinkers, astute businessmen — they were cut from the same stout cloth. Both were deeply patriotic Americans. They were profoundly Christian. Both believed that the best investment for the future was to provide a value-centered education for young people. Both were devoted husbands who shared their lives and their philanthropy with the two remarkable women who were present on this occasion.

Moved by their presence, Dr. Banowsky underscored the primary spiritual purpose of the college: "Five years ago, on May 23, 1970, as we broke the first ground for Seaver College, we pledged 'to bring together on these hills a community of scholars who hold distinctive spiritual beliefs.' Mr. Pepperdine had been a lifelong member of the Church of Christ, and the school's continuing relationship with its religious roots has created the core of its spiritual stance." Banowsky reinforced the commitment: "As we keep Christian values at the heart of the whole educational process, we will resist any sectarian spirit. We shall encourage full and open academic inquiry. What we affirm is that while our vision of truth is limited, ultimate truth actually exists. We affirm that the universe is undergirded by an objective moral order. We will continue to keep pace with change; but our main purpose, in this place, will be to discover what is not changing. And our central conviction will be that Jesus Christ is the same yesterday, today and forever.

"What we do here today, then, is of permanent importance. Perhaps no other institution of human creation is of such enduring quality as an institution of higher learning. Even nations and civilizations rise and fall while universities and colleges survive. Among the oldest continuing human creations are the great universities at Paris, Oxford and Cambridge which stretch back across the centuries to the 1100's. Harvard University was established in 1636, one hundred and forty years before the founding of the United States of America. During World War II when most of Germany was leveled by allied artillery, not one bomb was dropped on the beautiful city of Heidelberg because of its university. We believe that Seaver College of Pepperdine University will serve young people for centuries to come."

Continuing, Dr. Banowsky said, "In 1938 George Pepperdine chose as the motto of his university a verse of scripture: 'Freely ye received, freely give.' No person has more powerfully lived that truth than Blanche Ellen Theodora Ebert Seaver. Her middle name, Theodora, is my favorite. Of Greek derivation, it means, 'the gift of God.' I believe it is by the providence of God that Mrs. Seaver was brought into our lives."

As the ceremony neared its climax, Mrs. Frank Roger Seaver stood at the rostrum with Dr. Banowsky, one of the dearest friends of her lifetime, and briefly and simply acknowledged the naming of the college for her late husband. Its acceptance into the University family was verbalized by Mrs. George Pepperdine, who presented Mrs. Seaver with a copy of the founder's autobiography, *Faith Is My Fortune*. The two women embraced.

Dr. James W. Fifield, Jr., minister and friend of the Seavers for many years, read a Scripture. Dr. Howard H. White, executive vice-president of the university gave the dedicatory prayer.

Professor Stivers touched the keyboard of the organ for the recessional, "Jubilate."

The people, clad in academic robes, climbed back up the west stairway toward the complex of buildings now named — "from this day forward" — Frank R. Seaver College.

# 2

## A Native Son Is Born

When Richard C. Seaver discovered that Pepperdine College was mentioned in his uncle's will shortly after Frank Seaver's death in 1964, he called his Aunt Blanche. "What do you know about Pepperdine?" he asked her. "Not very much," she admitted. "Well," said Richard, "I don't either; but we'd better find out, because it was clearly important to Uncle Frank."

That was enough for Blanche Ebert Seaver. In her thorough way, she began to find out what made this small Christian college in Southwest Los Angeles important enough for her husband to remember it in his will.

She discovered that Frank Seaver and George Pepperdine had been contemporaries and had known each other in their early days as young businessmen in Los Angeles. She also discovered that Frank had taken a great interest in several programs initiated by Pepperdine College during the early 1960's, which without fanfare, he had supported financially. She knew that her husband, though one of the most generous supporters of independent higher education in California history, never treated such support lightly, no matter the size of the donation.

Blanche Seaver began to get acquainted with the Pepperdine administrators. She studied the academic and civic programs the school was engaged in and learned of further needs. What she found was a college bursting at its seams on a 33 acre campus, needing to expand, to reach for university status, to extend its influence as an independent, liberal arts, Christian institution.

Frank Roger Seaver lived a span of eighty-one eventful years. That the legacy he left, represented now in the college which bears his name, will far outlive the years of his life, partly reflects how this remarkable woman, with the trust her husband left in her keeping, added a truly amazing chapter to the annals of American higher education.

But the story began in San Jose where a train chugged into the station and stopped, its bell still clanging incessantly. Faces, faces filled with hope and curiosity, peered out through every window of the passenger cars. California! The word held a strange, exciting magic for these folk — pilgrims from other states come to claim a new life in answer to the land boom ads of speculators in the Golden State.

A newsboy, grimy and looking like anything but a son of some rich Californian (surely there could be no other kind!), came along the rickety boardwalk with an armload of papers, the *San Jose Daily Mercury*. The date was late in March, 1883, and the most prominent announcement on the front page (this being an era before headlines became important to peddling papers) was an advertisement for "S. Jacobs Oil, the great German remedy for pain" which promised cures for everything from lumbago to frostbite. A little weather story on the same page reported there had been a trace of rain but no frost in the area, and that the total fall for the season was fifteen inches of moisture.

There were other articles about a flood in Southern Russia, a potential revolution in Haiti, a cyclone in Arkansas and an article quoting Bishop Marty of Dakota as predicting that Sitting Bull would soon become a member of the Catholic Church.

Locally, there had been the commonplace thefts, a shooting, a citizen relieved of his wallet by a barmaid and the welcomed assurance that the notorious outlaw Joaquin Miller, was believed to be up in Oregon now, while Black Bart apparently had moved his road agency operations to the Lakeport area. There was even a story announcing the expected arrival of "three colonies of farmers, numbering 265 persons, from Colorado to buy land in this area and in Southern California."

The passengers began to alight, collect their baggage and hasten off to meet relatives, or begin their first day in their new home with no kin except those with them. Others, those planning to travel on south the next day, went to look for places to spend the night. Some stayed on the train to continue up the peninsula to San Francisco.

Carlton Seaver, a farmer from Iowa instead of Colorado, a serious man with a handsome brush mustache, waited in his pullman seat until the biggest rush had cleared the aisles. Then, solicitously, he helped his wife out of her seat and took the hand of the little girl, Georgia. Together they walked toward the exit. At the step, Carlton led the child down first and stood on one side, while the grinning porter stood on the other. Carefully, he assisted his wife to the platform beside the train, for she was with child.

A few days later, on April 12, 1883, in San Jose, California, Mary Estella Samuels Seaver proudly presented her husband with their second child and their first son. They named him Frank Roger Seaver.

As typical parents of first sons, this young farm couple, coming to California to seek their fortune, prayed that the infant would grow up to become a great American. They even harbored the hope that he might become a doctor.

Frank Roger Seaver didn't become a doctor. But his

parents did live long enough to see him become a great American citizen and to excel far beyond their grandest dreams.

Carlton Seaver himself was a God-fearing, courageous and industrious man of the stock from which pioneers are made. A native of New York, he was married in Iowa to another New Yorker, Mary Estella Samuels, who was of the same sort of sturdy stock. Together they were fitted perfectly to the making of the frontier that was Southern California in the early 1880s.

Carlton Seaver knew what he wanted. He wanted land — land with water so that he could farm. He wanted to be a part of a progressive community where he could adequately provide for his young family and give them the grounding they needed to strike out on their own, once he had done his part.

Two weeks after Frank was born in San Jose, the family moved on southward and arrived in the storied City of the Angels, then a sprawling community of 20,000 people. But Los Angeles was not Carlton Seaver's final destination.

Alighting from the train at the Southern Pacific Depot, the Seavers immediately encountered the feverish boom that the railroads had created. "Boosters," as the land speculators were called, paraded up and down the railroad platform with huge billboards picturing beautiful vineyards, orchards and homes in new subdivisions scattered throughout the Los Angeles basin.

Estella Seaver pressed the blanket more tightly about the ears of the infant in her arms as the blare of a Booster band started, and with it the shouts of a land huckster offering prime property at bargain prices.

"Let's get out of here," Carlton Seaver said, taking his wife's arm in one hand and leading the child, Georgia, with the other.

This was not where Carlton Seaver wanted to settle.

Collecting their luggage, the Seavers hired a horse-drawn hack and moved along the dusty streets of Los Angeles toward busy Spring Street, where they would stay temporarily in a hotel. The astonishing sight which greeted them, a huge traffic jam the entire length of the street, has never been entirely untangled to this day. Every type of mule and horse-powered vehicle imaginable — wagons, buggies, buckboards, hacks, trolleys — were milling around, seemingly in utter confusion. Fearless pedestrians wove their way through the undulating mass of humanity. Mrs. Seaver clutched her precious bundle tightly as their driver somehow maneuvered his way to their hotel.

The next day, promising his family he would return as soon as he could, Carlton Seaver caught the train out to Pomona, the eastern terminus of the Southern Pacific, (soon to be hooked up with the Santa Fe coming in from the East).

This is what had brought the great boom to Southern California — the railroads. Wherever the rail lines stretched, land became precious and towns sprang up. The railroads had accomplished overnight what the Boosters had been unable to do for several years with their great promotional schemes, with their praise for Southern California's climate, soil and opportunities.

It had only been two years before the Seavers arrived that one such scheme had backfired. Angelenos had succeeded in persuading the California Editors Association to conduct its annual convention in Los Angeles in early 1881, so that newsmen from all over the state, including those whose dispatches reached the wealthy in the Middlewest and the East, would report that the balmy winter climate and all of the other wild claims were gospel. But something closely resembling icicles hung from the eaves of buildings in Los Angeles that fateful first night of the convention. The next morning, the entire Southland was blanketed with a light snow! Despite the cries of Angelenos that this was "very unusual" weather, all of the out-of-town editors wrote to their hometown papers that Los Angeles was just like any other California town, except it was populated by an unusually heavy concentration of liars.

Then, not long afterward, the rails came, and it was like the Gold Rush all over again. The main difference was that most of the newcomers were substantial citizens with the means to buy land.

That was the category in which Carlton Seaver belonged, and it didn't take him long to find the land he wanted, not far from the bustling little village of Claremont. Uncleared except for a homesite in the middle of a newly planted orange grove with walnut, fig, prune and other fruit trees, the land stretched along what is now Foothill Boulevard through Claremont.

Here Carlton Seaver built a small ranch home for his family and started clearing off the tangled, sage-covered acres so he could plant fruit-bearing trees and other crops. Here, in this wonderful, open land, young Frank Seaver spent his early years, romping freely over the fields and orchards, doing his share of the chores when he was old enough. His body grew strong and his mind was bright. It was from this rural home that Frank and Georgia trudged to classes at the first little Claremont School, located in a store building facing the railroad tracks, where one young man taught five grades with a total enrollment of some twenty boys and girls.

Frank was about nine when his parents decided to move into the larger community of Pomona. Frank's father decided to move for two reasons: he and his wife felt they needed to be nearer better schools for their growing family, and Carlton Seaver saw a new career opportunity — banking — in the larger town. So, in 1892, the family moved into a big, comfortable, white-pillared home on Holt Avenue in

Pomona and Carlton Seaver soon established the First National Bank, later to be absorbed by the United California Bank. He continued his farming activities, served as president of the bank for many years, and became one of the leading citizens of the community.

From the great home on Holt Avenue, which became a mecca for classmates of the Seaver youngsters, Frank, his eldest sister Georgia, and the four other children who came along later, went off to the schools of Pomona eventually to become successful in their chosen fields.

Following Georgia and Frank in the family were Byron Dick, Homer Carlton, Marguerite and Nila.

Although Carlton Seaver had wanted Frank to become a doctor, he became a lawyer instead. The father then encouraged Byron Dick to study medicine, but this son also became a successful attorney. It was the third boy, Homer Carlton, who finally became the one to fulfill his father's dream of having a physician in the family.

As for the Claremont ranch which the elder Seaver operated until shortly before his death in 1927, part of it later became a portion of the campus of Pomona College, the institution which played such a significant role in the life of Frank Roger Seaver and which he repaid so handsomely as one of the school's most generous alumni.

# 3

## A Leader in the Wilderness

A beautiful Friday in June of 1903, found the entire membership of the "Knights of the Dagger" packing up for a weekend hike into the nearby San Gabriel Mountains. The Greek letters, Kappa Delta, standing for a fraternity at Pomona College which to this day attracts top college athletes, stood for a somewhat more romantically labeled order back there three years into the Twentieth Century. The terrain was near the string of communities blossoming along the railroad from Los Angeles toward San Bernardino. But that didn't make the rugged reaches of the ageless hills any less formidable.

Walking north from the young Pomona College campus, already becoming beautifully shaded by fine specimens of fir, pine, cedar, oak, eucalyptus, elm, palm, and sycamore, it did not take the Knights long to realize that the slope was a lot steeper and more densely covered with brush than was apparent to the eye from a distance. These strong young men, all athletes, met the challenge with sturdy legs and healthy lungs, which not only could bear the burden of the climb, but could still shout the exuberant shouts of carefree youth on a weekend outing.

The range toward which the young men hiked continued to appear deceptively serene. The first range they approached was called the San Jose Hills. Behind them loomed the San

Gabriel Mountain Range, now a part of the Angeles National Forest, with rugged old Mount Baldy the predominant feature of the whole scene.

Walking with as much ease and enthusiasm as the rest of the twenty or so members of the Knights, but making scarcely as much noise as the others, was Frank Roger Seaver. Without overtly seeking the role, he had already been accepted as the leader for the outing. Nobody had suggested that a vote be taken and that Frank, as the man who knew the area best, who had practically grown up in these hills which shadowed his home, be the leader. It just seemed natural to turn to him, and that's the way it happened. So, when the group came to the first rise of the San Jose Hills, a steep, sage-covered one, they stopped and looked questioningly at Frank Seaver.

"That way," he said, pointing east, and the group turned to skirt the base of the hill.

By this time they were about three miles from the Pomona campus. Soon they came to the wide entrance to San Antonio Canyon, and here Frank directed them north again. Mount Baldy looked benevolently down on them from its lofty height and beckoned the party up its timbered slopes.

Now the climb became steeper and, as they warmed, the fellows started to perspire. Soon they were shedding the jackets and sweaters they had needed in the early morning chill. Tucking the garments into the packs on their backs, they hiked along the rocky banks of San Antonio Creek, rushing clear and cool along its steep boulder-filled bed, and providing a source for replenishing the quickly emptying canteens the boys carried on their hips. The hills began to rise higher on either side of the creek as the canyon narrowed and soon the smaller brush of the hills was replaced by trees — evergreens, oaks and, nearer the water, the cottonwoods.

By noontime, the Knights were within sight of the

Pomona Water Power Plant. The facility, which is no longer in existence, was built in 1892 by the San Antonio Power Company, organized by Dr. Cyrus G. Galdwin, then president of Pomona College. Here, below the plant, Frank called a halt for a rest and renewal of energy from the lunch they had packed.

"We could have come along that road," one of the Knights complained half-seriously to Frank, pointing to the horse trail on the other side of the creek leading up to the power plant.

"We could have," Frank admitted, "but what kind of a hike would that be?"

For any lad who had qualified for membership in a fraternity called Knights of the Dagger, that question was, of course, rhetorical. The fellow who was asked it grinned.

After the picnic the young men, some of them wet to the knees from frolicking in the stream while they were supposed to be resting, started on up the canyon. They exchanged cheerful greetings with the caretaker as they passed the power plant.

Two or three miles above the plant the Knights hiked into a large bowl in the canyon. Here they found a beaver dam, a sandy beach and a natural park of great trees coming almost to the water. On each side of the canyon were taller trees and a veritable forest just to the north of them, which today provides the picturesque setting for some small ranches and the colorful little Mount Baldy Village.

"Let's camp here," Frank Seaver suggested. There was plenty of time yet before dark to set up camp and gather wood for fires to cook their evening meal. That night, and the two following days and nights, the little valley rang with laughter and shouts and songs of a happy bunch of young men living it up in the wilds. It seemed a long way from the routine of their classes at Pomona College.

With reluctance, they began to break camp on Monday

Lt. Frank R. Seaver is seen with his shipmates in the bottom row, at the far right, during World War I Naval service.

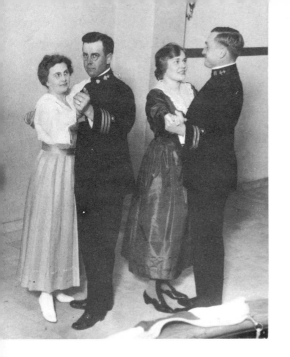

Memorable pictures from Frank's service in the Navy. In the top left, he dances with Blanche shortly after their marriage.

Above, a scene in San Francisco during the great earthquake. Frank Seaver was on patrol duty here with the National Guard. Below, kneeling at right, he is shown with Glenn Martin and others at a meeting of the Aviation Section of the California Naval Militia, which Frank helped pioneer.

Frank was a member of the football team at Pomona College. He is shown here over the ball in practice in 1902.

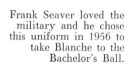

Frank Seaver loved the military and he chose this uniform in 1956 to take Blanche to the Bachelor's Ball.

morning for the return trip down the canyon and back to civilization. As it turned out, three of the group decided to prolong the adventure by going back a different route.

"Just follow the creek," Frank Seaver instructed the main party, "and you can't possibly get lost. You'll be back by mid-afternoon, because it's much faster going down. Tell anyone who needs to know that we should be back by dark or soon after."

"If we don't get lost," quipped Roy Thomas, who was later to become a successful physician and Frank Seaver's brother-in-law. He spoke more prophetically than he realized.

With Frank and Roy as they separated from the group was Carl Parker, later a prominent radiologist in Pasadena. The trio had decided to make the trip home a little more challenging by climbing the steep ridge west of their camp-site, dropping down into San Dimas Canyon and returning to the Pomona Valley by way of Laverne.

The climb up the first wall of the canyon was bad enough. It was worse going down the other side, as they found themselves in terrain which had apparently not been penetrated at all by man, and very little by beast. The brush was so thick, prickly and unyielding that they had to fight their way virtually every inch down the sheer slope into the canyon hundreds of feet below.

Frank Seaver found himself looking frequently with mild misgivings at the wall on the other side which, if anything, appeared worse than the one they were now descending. He also began to notice that the wall seemed to completely enclose the canyon to form a deep, elongated bowl in the hills.

"Boy," said one of the other fellows at one point, "I'll be just as glad when we get to the bottom and can head on down the canyon."

"Where," Frank asked, dryly, "do you see the canyon going down between any hills?"

The boys stopped.

"What does that mean, Frank?" Roy asked.

"It means this is a box canyon that doesn't lead anywhere, much less into San Dimas Canyon," Frank correctly diagnosed. "The only way out is the same way we're going in — by climbing."

Roy whistled.

"We're almost at the bottom. Let's go on down and see if we can't find a little easier place to climb out than this," Frank said.

It was approaching nightfall before they found what appeared to be a not so rugged hillside. It was only a bit farther north of the very place they had come into the box canyon. This meant, of course, they would have to climb back to where they had started from when they left the other Knights.

"So, we'll go back to San Antonio Canyon, instead of San Dimas," Frank concluded, not too disappointedly.

"We'd better hurry," said Carl, glancing anxiously at the sun settling into the horizon.

But Frank Seaver knew it would be foolish to get caught on those treacherous slopes at night.

"We'll have to camp here overnight," he announced.

"Our folks will surely be worried," Roy reminded.

"I know it," Frank conceded, "but they'd be more worried if we all broke our necks trying to get out of here in the dark. Besides, my parents know I wouldn't try anything that stupid up here, and they'll most likely figure out exactly what's happened."

The boys then remembered another small problem. They were without food, every morsel having been hungrily devoured as scheduled in the weekend campout. Of course, hardy as they were, lack of food for another day would not have unduly harmed them. But, being hungry, adventurous, and with some daylight left, they decided to search for something edible in the canyon. What they finally found was a pool of water which apparently had its source of supply in a spring trickling down through the rocky innards of the hillside. What they also found was a sizable turtle basking on the banks of the small pond. Mr. Turtle, thanks to Frank Seaver's skills as an outdoorsman, soon became turtle soup with plenty of rich, tasty meat to appease the ravenous appetites of the trio. With full stomachs, they slept like logs under the open skies that night.

The next day, Tuesday, was anti-climactic. Going back up the hill at the less treacherous place they had discovered the night before, they soon were at the crest of the ridge and then were sliding happily down a pathway of loose shale into San Antonio Canyon.

The search party from Claremont had barely organized and started up toward the canyon, when the three missing Knights of the Dagger came charging out of the hills. It was a joyful reunion. As Frank Seaver predicted, his parents, though naturally worried, had already figured out that the boys weren't really lost, only delayed a while.

# 4

## A Youth of Strong Character

Frank Seaver's leadership during his fraternity days at Pomona began to develop long before he became a college student. Even as an unusually quiet and serious child he excelled in games and assumed a role of leadership in a culture where children often had to invent their own pastimes.

Boyhood classmates always remembered the big Seaver house on Holt Avenue as the place where they gathered for their activities — first for play as children, and later as the meeting place for high school and college affairs. They also remembered Frank's mother as the kind of woman equal to all occasions, hospitable, and never upset by the number of other young people her sizable brood brought home with them. Remembering Mary Seaver, Frank M. Taylor, one of Frank's Pomona College classmates once said, "I've always had the feeling that successful men draw strength from their mothers and I think this was true of Frank Seaver."

In high school Frank not only made good grades but continued to develop his leadership capacity as a member of the Pomona High School Cadets. It was in this organization that he received his first taste of military discipline which he was to love throughout his life. He used his love of the outdoors to move rapidly up the leadership ladder to the rank of captain. He often led his squad in elaborate drills on the field and took pride in its ability and precision. Even before the Knights of the Dagger adventure, Frank once accompanied the High School Cadets on a hike all the way from Pomona to Laguna Beach, a distance which would be a challenge even to more professional military men. To later master the night in the box canyon so calmly and lightly was no great wonder.

Graduating from Pomona High in the Spring of 1901, Frank became a freshman at Pomona College in the fall of the same year. Fellow students were not long in recognizing the strength, intelligence and leadership abilities of this quiet and serious fellow student. On November 7, 1901, scarcely two months after Frank Seaver enrolled at Pomona, the freshman class conducted an election of officers. Frank Seaver was elected treasurer. He became a Knight of the Dagger early in his freshman year, being initiated during a meeting in his own home.

As a sophomore, Frank Seaver became a member of the Debating Club and was soon elected secretary-treasurer. The October 23, 1903 issue of *Student Life* reported, "At the football rally on Friday night, Frank Seaver, manager of the team, gave one of the stirring speeches." Later issues of the publication told of the football team manager making "flying trips" here and there, from Los Angeles to Riverside, making arrangements for games.

On June 10, 1904, a new Constitution of the Associated Students of Pomona College was adopted. Shortly afterward, the first annual election under the Constitution was conducted; 111 votes were cast and Frank Roger Seaver emerged as the president.

A hint of the direction toward which young Frank was looking for his career in life was contained in this excerpt from the March 24, 1905 issue of *Student Life*: "Pomona College Debating Club sat as the Superior Court of the

County of Los Angeles, Dept. 3, to try James Iouswine for assault with intent to do injury. Frank R. Seaver and W. C. Eherle acted as attorneys for the defendant. The jury could not agree, resulting in the calling of a new trial."

Other items in *Student Life* and the *Metate* during Frank Seaver's junior and senior years, portray his energies in the Intercollegiate Oratorical Association, as managing editor of the *Metate*, as a member of the Science Club, treasurer of the Pomona College Athletic Association, member of the Sirocco Fraternity as well as Kappa Delta, and a member of the Biological Seminar.

One other important event in the college life of Frank Seaver was hearing Teddy Roosevelt speak on campus. Here, indeed, was a kindred soul; a man noted for his love of the outdoor life, a great military figure, and a man of politics, an area which intrigued Frank Seaver all his life. He later said that this exposure to Teddy Roosevelt was what probably convinced him to go into law and even make a couple of forays into politics, once as an unsuccessful candidate for the State Legislature, and the second time, in a successful and significant race for the Board of Freeholders of Los Angeles County.

Aside from his college activities, and probably because of his eventual career as a High School Cadet, Frank joined the National Guard while a student at Pomona. Taking his first summer training at Atascadero in 1903, he spent three years in the Guard, and this career was marked by first hand experience in a drama of historic significance. This came following the great San Francisco earthquake and fire which almost destroyed the city on the hills by the Golden Gate. Frank and his unit were ordered to active policing duties in San Francisco following that disaster. For a month he was part of the force which patrolled the desolate, rubble-choked streets with loaded rifles and orders to shoot to kill if they came across any looting or similar disorder.

That experience in San Francisco came not long after Frank Seaver received his degree as a member of the twelfth graduating class of Pomona College. While the memorable tour of guard duty in the quake-ravaged city cut into his post-graduate year of reading law, Frank passed his bar examination with flying colors and was admitted to legal practice in the Fall of 1906. Then, with his customary thoroughness, he followed that milestone with a year of study at Harvard Law School as a special student who had already passed the bar. Later, in 1913, this foresight paid off when Frank Seaver was admitted to the practice of the law before the Supreme Court of the United States.

Frank Seaver never had an opportunity to try a case before the Supreme Court and had little desire to do so. But he had a unique philosophy about being prepared for anything. Therefore, to satisfy himself, if he was to be a lawyer at all, he reasoned that he had to be prepared to practice before the highest court in the land! Frank Seaver had that kind of determination about everything he did.

Shortly after he arrived at Harvard, Frank wrote a letter home which revealed something else about his developing personality — a respect for money. In his letter he was telling the folks about wanting to visit Niagara Falls on his way back to Cambridge. But he had been warned that cab drivers had the habit of charging ten cents to take a passenger out to the Falls and ten dollars to bring him back. "So I walked!" he concluded practically.

If Frank Seaver learned respect for money at an early age, he showed his generosity even earlier. He developed a remarkable appreciation for his educational opportunities and held his professors at Pomona in the highest esteem. He saw them as men and women completely dedicated to a single purpose, the sharing of knowledge with the young. So impressed was this young man with the obvious devotion of these learned professors that he felt compelled to repay his Alma Mater in a material way for the education he was receiving. How he expressed it was unique in the annals of the young college. As a junior or senior student, Frank took out a life insurance policy for the then staggering face value of $30,000 — and made Pomona College the beneficiary!

For the next six decades Frank Seaver multiplied his original donation many times. If he could have had his way, it all would have been done completely without fanfare.

# 5

## Frank R. Seaver--Attorney at Law

This trip by train from Pomona to Los Angeles in the fall of 1907 was nothing new to Frank R. Seaver; he had made it many times before. But this time his reason for making the trip was different.

He looked out the window as the train labored up the grade to drop over into the San Gabriel Valley. His eyes were on the barren hills, parched brown from the lack of rain this season, but his mind was on his destination and the beginning of his career in law.

When the train arrived at the Los Angeles depot, he jumped off, bought a newspaper and started walking to the hotel where he had already made reservations for temporary quarters as he started his new job. He knew he'd soon have to find modest room and board — modest because his position with the law office of George Sanders only offered him twenty-five dollars a month. But Frank Seaver wasn't worried, mainly because he had every confidence that he would soon be earning more than that. In fact, he was already looking toward the day when he would have his own law practice.

The newspaper under his arm contained assurances that Los Angeles was a very likely place for a promising young attorney to seek fame and fortune. The town was booming. Construction of new buildings was keeping pace with last year's boom. George T. Cline, a native of Los Angeles who had made a fortune as a Chicago businessman, was back home buying up real estate along Broadway at $5400 a front foot and paying "spot cash" for several parcels of partially developed downtown real estate. Increased activity in foreign shipping into Los Angeles ports was being hailed as "only a foretaste of what the future holds in store." Mayor Harper was trying to get more municipal revenue, and his current campaign was to increase the taxes from one dollar to three dollars a month on street lunchstands.

Even the national and world situation looked pretty good. Teddy Roosevelt, now in his second term as President and hotly disclaiming any desire to seek a third, was stumping about the country on behalf of Republicans in the off-year election. The tour apparently proved very effective since many GOP sweeps, including "Old Kentucky," were recorded that November. All this news about his favorite president intrigued young Seaver, especially since it included detailed plans for a bear hunting expedition which the president was about to take into the canebreak country of Louisiana.

Not even Japan's sword-rattling sounded too ominous. The news dispatches were reporting that the Japanese people cheered mightily when Secretary of War Taft declared in a ringing speech in Tokyo that "war between the two nations would be criminal."

As for the local situation, just one day's synopsis of the news on the front page of the paper would be enough to convince an enterprising young attorney that his prospects were bright. The synopsis, with a familiar ring to more modern times, read: "Crowded city awes Indian squaw; feared to pass through jammed streets . . . body of Chester Silent found in lake . . . five hundred empty whiskey bottles found in County Jail, legacy of a former administration

. . . squabble over hogs stirs Vernon . . . spite fence fails to end war of San Marino . . . state delves into 'mallet cure' death case . . . lively tiff between attorneys in Santa Fe rebate fight . . . clubman who stayed away nights finds wife gone and house stripped . . . city officials want larger charter revision commission . . . United States Treasury officials here on visit; look lightly on stock slump . . . man charged with mayhem on trial after fight of five years . . . local hunters pay well for hunt in British Columbia . . . Forty-Niner commits suicide . . . real estate man arrested on serious charges, breaks into slang . . . big attendance hears pointed saying at Baptist convention . . . woman stricken with ptomaine poisoning after eating candy . . ."

Such was the news in Los Angeles when Frank Roger Seaver arrived in 1907 to begin his career in law.

To no one's great surprise, he did well. Six months after his arrival, he quit his salaried job and hung up his own shingle, opening his law offices in the Hollingsworth Building. Frank was joined shortly after that by his brother, Byron Dick, who had just graduated from Pomona in the spring of 1908. The brothers practiced together until Frank decided to go on to greater things almost a decade later. Byron Dick continued to practice law at the same address until his death in 1954.

Frank Roger Seaver quickly became a successful lawyer, a young man about town residing in the University Club and active in many cultural and civic affairs. He belonged to the Amateur Players Club, taking part in its productions, and served in 1910 as president. It was, in fact, his connection with this club which eventually led him to the one and only romance of his life. In 1910, he served as president of the Pomona College Alumni Association. In 1912, he was elected to the Board of Freeholders of Los Angeles County, a board which drafted the first Los Angeles County charter.

Probably few local governments in the country have had as significant a basic document. It is not a lengthy document, nor is it couched in terms that only the legal mind can understand. The most astounding thing about the Los Angeles County Charter is that it exists today almost word for word just as it was drafted sixty years ago. The few minor changes that were made a half century after it was originally drafted were done by a specially appointed commission which included Frank R. Seaver, as the sole surviving member of the Board of Freeholders. He was credited with being the genius behind the drafting of the charter, and the one who almost singlehandedly wrote it.

To jump ahead of this story, Frank Seaver answered his telephone one day in 1952 to take a call from Second District Supervisor Kenneth Hahn, now the senior member of the county governing board.

"Aren't you the Frank Seaver who helped draw up the County charter?" Hahn inquired.

"I am," Mr. Seaver admitted.

Hahn explained that the Board of Supervisors had authorized a special celebration to commemorate the 40th Anniversary of the charter and to honor the two surviving members of the Board of Freeholders, Frank Seaver and Willis Booth.

The 40th Anniversary was a nice affair. But the 50th Anniversary celebration, staged by Hahn ten years later, was even more impressive. By that time, Frank, then in his late seventies, was the only surviving Freeholder.

The 50th Charter Anniversary celebration in 1962 started with a parade from the Seaver home on an exceptionally brisk morning. It was so cold that Blanche and Frank were kept busy for a while running from closet to closet to dig out extra coats and sweaters for the many guests who had not come adequately dressed for this kind of parade. The kind of parade it turned out to be was a ride all the way to the county building in a caravan of vintage autos of fifty years of age. Most of these, of course, were open touring cars. It was quite a parade, though, and received a lot of attention from passers-by.

Dr. Rufus von KleinSmid, chancellor of the University of Southern California and devoted friend and neighbor of the Seavers, made a speech. Frank responded. Kenny Hahn presented Frank with a 50-year-old ink well set as a memento of the occasion.

The program was capped off and, as it turned out, livened up considerably, when the Governor's call from Sacramento came through. The phone was connected to the loud speaker system so all attending could hear the two-way conversations between Governor Edmund G. (Pat) Brown, a staunch Democrat, and the Seavers, staunch Republicans.

Several dignitaries spoke to the Governor, including Frank Seaver, who returned polite thanks for Brown's congratulations. Then someone shoved the phone into Blanche Seaver's not so willing hands before she could say "yea" or "nay" to their hurried: "You want to speak to the Governor?"

"I hear you are a good Republican," Governor Brown started out heartily, and made what Blanche felt were a few barbed remarks about her party affiliation.

Never one to hide her thoughts, Blanche responded with partisan enthusiasm and a political donnybrook between a Democratic Governor and a lady Republican appeared about to erupt. Brown, aware he had met his match, or conscious that the conversation was being amplified before the press, backed down and laughingly suggested they not start a "little spat."

It was shortly after the memorable 50th Charter Anniversary celebration that Frank Seaver was appointed to a special commission to review the Charter to see if it could

33

be improved or needed to be updated. The committee met for long hours every Tuesday night for eight months. The conclusion finally reached was that the commission could find no way to improve the classic document, a real tribute to the young attorney who helped author it.

Meanwhile, to return to Frank Seaver's years as a young attorney, 1912 was a busy year for him in many ways. In addition to his impressive civic and social activities, he returned to his love of the military, joining the California Naval Militia. Going in as a Seaman Second Class, he moved up to the rank of Ensign in a brief period, and in 1914 became a Lieutenant in command of the newly formed Ninth Division which he had helped to organize.

As a member of the Naval Militia, Frank took three-week military cruises each summer on the cruiser *Marblehead*, the torpedo boat *Farragut*, and the destroyers *Hopkins* and *Hull*. He also took part in frequent weekend cruises for drilling the gun crews, practicing navigation and other nautical drills and duties. This, coupled with later wartime duty in the Navy, instilled in young Seaver an abiding love for the sea and seamanship. With his usual ambition to master anything he undertook, it is not surprising that he later studied intensively until he could pass the qualifying examinations for the rank of Master Mariner in the Merchant Marine. This made him eligible to command ocean-going vessels of any kind on any of the world's seas. Frank Seaver never did put this accomplishment to use; it simply reflects the same kind of determination he showed in qualifying to practice before the United States Supreme Court.

Frank Seaver not only loved the military, he was far-sighted enough to see that his beloved country was heading toward a day in history when her young men needed to be prepared with such training. By 1915 World War I had started in Europe and Frank was among those who felt the United States would become involved before it was over.

In this same period he became interested in aviation, that exciting innovation which was by then a part of war in the skies over Europe.

Believing that aviation had a place in the future of America's military might, Frank Seaver put his legal training and organizational experience to work. He succeeded in obtaining a permit in 1915 to establish the Aviation Section of the California Naval Militia, one of the first such organizations in the country. Two airplanes were supplied to the unit by the United States Government. The men received their instruction at the State Armory in Los Angeles' Exposition Park and their flight training at Gardena Aviation Field.

Lieutenant Seaver never learned to fly. He was too busy as the founder of the group. The flight training was provided by Glenn Martin and members of his school and factory staff.

Thus did Frank Seaver help his country as war threatened and at the same time prepared himself to serve when it finally came.

One friendship with a fellow member of the Naval Reserves which developed during this training was with Ned Doheny, and his father, oilman Edward L. Doheny, who was around to give a hand in the new aviation group. The Doheny friendship was later to have a profound impact on the life of Frank Roger Seaver.

# 6

## The Girl of His Dreams

That morning in 1915, Militia Lt. Frank R. Seaver had been up long before daylight to be at Gardena Aviation Field to help check out daring young pilots for their licenses.

Later that afternoon, Lawyer Frank Seaver and a client were riding along the bumpy Hill Street trolley. The young attorney's attention was suddenly distracted from the business at hand when a beautiful young lady got aboard.

His heart did great flip-flops, he later admitted, and the only thing that kept him from leaping off the streetcar when she departed three blocks from where she boarded was the presence of the important client.

That was the exact moment when Frank Roger Seaver, long noted as a handsome and eligible young bachelor with more interest in his work and military duties than the opposite sex, was smitten by the vision of loveliness which he had seen for only a few moments on a Los Angeles streetcar. The vision persisted in his mind. Soon he confided to his good friend, Allen Archer, that he had seen the girl of his dreams but did not have the slightest idea who she was or where he could find her.

Allen Archer listened sympathetically, unaware that destiny was providing an important role for him to play in this drama.

Several weeks later the two friends, both members of

the Amateur Players Club, attended a rehearsal in Banning's barn on Adams Street, of Gilbert and Sullivan's "Patience." They had scarcely stepped into the old building, long since gone, when the not-quite-so-patient Frank Seaver spotted The Girl as she walked in promptly at eight o'clock.

"That's the girl!" he whispered excitedly to Allen Archer, his voice awed by the reappearance of the vision which had become so much a part of his dreams the past few weeks. "That's the girl I've been telling you about for weeks!"

"Miss Ebert?" was Allen's surprising response. "Why, that's Miss Blanche Ebert, the new vocal coach who has moved here from Chicago."

"You know her?" Frank pressed.

"Why, sure. I'll introduce you. Nothing easier."

It was not as easy as Allen Archer pretended. She was extremely busy that first night. And Allen Archer, who really didn't have a speaking acquaintance with the young lady, began to get cold feet with so much activity and so many people milling about. Both quickly guessed, from the manner of the young woman, that she was a proud and proper person, not easily approached in such a situation. Strategy, then, seemed called for and reluctantly the pair finally left. Frank was sad over the fact that an introduction had not taken place but glad that he at least knew the identity of The Girl.

True to his noble standard of friendship, Allen Archer, who died several years before Frank's passing, vowed to his friend that he would find a way to bring about a proper introduction.

"Do it!" Frank urged.

The way Allen managed it was unique and required what amounted to considerable sacrifice on his part in the name of friendship. He called Miss Ebert at her studio in Blanchard Hall in downtown Los Angeles. He did not mention Frank Seaver. What he did mention was a pretended burning ambition to learn to play the piano.

That was the business Miss Ebert was in. "What did you say your name was?" inquired Miss Ebert, all business.

"Allen Archer," he said. "You know me from the Amateur Players."

When the name repeated and connected with the Players still obviously didn't register with the young woman, Archer could not resist kidding her a little.

"I'm the fat fellow," he said, "Short and fat."

Blanche Seaver still laughs about it today. "When he did show up for that first lesson I couldn't help but laugh when he came in. He wasn't short and fat at all. He was tall, lean, and handsome."

Allen played his role perfectly, although it did not take Miss Ebert long to discover that his talent for music was more imagined than real. She still did not suspect his real motive and heroically tried for several weeks to help the struggling young man through the initial lessons.

Finally, he one day dropped Frank Seaver's name in a casual way, just mentioning him as his best friend. It seemed only natural to Miss Ebert that the name would come up occasionally after that as this personable student of hers talked of things about himself and his best friend. So it came as no sudden surprise to her when one day, after eight weeks of twice-a-week piano lessons, Allen Archer mildly suggested that he would like for her to meet Frank Seaver. There seemed no particular reason to avoid such a simple request and she agreed without thinking much about it.

Once the introduction came off, Frank Seaver needed no other encouragement. He asked her for a date. She accepted. He took her to Del Monico's for dinner. She enjoyed it. She accepted other similar invitations to go out with the young attorney. She enjoyed these. It even took her a while to begin to wonder why Allen Archer suddenly stopped taking piano lessons and when she finally did figure it out it was too late. But, unlike the smitten young lawyer, Blanche Ebert had not been immediately swept off her feet.

"When I came to love Frank," she reflected a decade after his death, "I couldn't possibly tell you. It came so gradually and it was built on respect for his kindness, his knowledge, his thoughfulness and so many other things about his personality and character that were good."

But love did indeed come to Blanche Ebert. When it did, it was profound. Time proved they both knew their own hearts.

They became engaged on June 30, 1916. And on September 16, 1916, Miss Blanche Ellen Theodora Ebert and Frank Roger Seaver were united in marriage in Chicago's North Shore Congregational Church.

The selection of Chicago as the place for the wedding was made because that was the bride's home throughout her childhood and all her family still lived there.

Blanche was the youngest of ten children of Mr. and Mrs. Theodore Ebert. Both of her parents were born in Bergen, Norway, and had immigrated to Chicago when they were children. Growing up in this large, happy and closely-knit family, especially as the youngest, affectionately nicknamed "Lovey," taught Blanche many things about thrift, the virtue of hard work, doing one's share and many other worthy attributes which contributed to a happy marriage, and which have remained with her throughout her life. Blanche's father established Theo. Ebert & Company, a painting and decorating business, in 1873. The business is still flourishing and in the family, now headed by Theodore Ebert III as president.

It was in Chicago that Blanche learned to play the piano when she was so small she had to be lifted onto the stool. In fact, she was still in kindergarten when she was "discovered." It happened one day when the kindergarten teacher, Miss Shelton, announced that the students would not be able to sing their little songs of the morning because the teacher who played the piano was ill.

"I can play the songs," piped up a small voice.

The voice belonged to a tiny blonde-haired girl by the name of Blanche Ebert. To the teacher's complete surprise, she did play the songs! So well did the child perform, that her impressed teacher walked home with her when school was out.

"Do you realize," the teacher told little Blanche's parents, "that you have a most unusual child?"

They looked perplexed.

"I mean her music," Miss Shelton went on.

"Oh, we all play and sing in this household," the teacher was assured. "We have thought nothing special of Blanche's talents."

Miss Shelton persisted, convinced there was something special about the little girl. She explained that she herself had been taking singing lessons at Jane Addams' famous Hull House.

"I wish you'd let me take Blanche down there with me so the piano teacher could hear her play," Miss Shelton urged.

The parents saw nothing wrong with that and gave their permission. As it turned out, her teacher was right. Blanche so impressed some of Chicago's finest teachers at the audition — Miss Eleain Smith, Miss Honey and Jane Addams — that transportation was arranged to bring her to Hull House twice every week for lessons. By the time she was thirteen the young pianist had pupils of her own at Hull House, and soon she was becoming a much sought after accompanist, vocal coach and concert pianist.

Her first trip to California was in September of 1912, and the idea of her going so far to such a savage land caused

Blanche Ebert Seaver — the girl of his dreams.

Eyes only for each other.

Blanche gave up a musical
career for her Frank . . .

. . . but the piano has always
remained an important part
of her life.

considerable concern to her parents and her brothers. They reluctantly agreed to a survey trip to investigate the opportunities for a budding young musician. She was enchanted with the warm Southern California climate and before long made her second trip to the West Coast. On the third trip she stayed to begin her own career. She opened a studio in the Majestic Building and later moved it to Blanchard Hall where she was "discovered" the second time, this time by her husband-to-be.

Blanche Ebert was well on her way as a blossoming celebrity before she met Frank Seaver. Her name and photograph were appearing with increasing frequency on the society pages of Los Angeles newspapers.

"The piano solo by Miss Blanche Ebert," commented one critic in 1914, concerning a concert of the Whittier Choral Society, "was one of the best numbers of the evening."

"Miss Blanche Ebert played the accompaniments for Mr. Seiling, and she deserves the greatest amount of praise for her sympathetic work," said another reviewer of another program.

On and on it went. Her name began to be linked to Estelle Heartt Dreyfus in many musical programs in which Blanche was the accompanist for the famed contralto. She played in concert with violin virtuoso Ignaz Haroldi. Among the long list of other artists she became associated with before her marriage were Oskar Seiling, Louise Rieger, Anna Kopetsky, Louise Gunning, Marie B. Tiffany, Axel Simonson, Juan de la Cruz, Anthony Carlson, Ettore Campana, Marguerite Stevenson, Fred Ellis and others.

A keen insight of Blanche Seaver's philosophy about her own work was contained in a feature story in the January 15, 1914, edition of the *Los Angeles Daily Tribune*. Because this unknown writer expressed it so beautifully and because the thoughts still portray so much of the intense feelings of Mrs. Seaver, the entire 1914 article demands to be recaptured:

"In her studio in the Blanchard building, Miss Blanche Ebert talked yesterday concerning her music, her ambitions and her aims.

"Miss Ebert is an unusual young woman, for she has grasped the significance and beauty of life as it is — not as it appears on the surface.

" 'Life is short, but art is long.'

"Thus does Miss Ebert epigrammatically and tersely quote what she is trying to accomplish — an expression of the true art of music.

" 'I am studying as well as teaching and accompanying on the piano,' said Miss Ebert. 'I am trying to express the compositions of the masters of music, but it requires many things to do this — command of the languages, feeling, sympathy, suffering, joy and above everything else the great desire to express music, not merely to play the piano, but to become a master of the instrument, to be able and worthy to comprehend the souls of the musicians who received the gift of music from the Greatest Musician.

" 'When I was a child of five years in a Chicago kindergarten my teachers discovered that I had talent. When one of them happened to be absent one day, I said, 'let me play the march she plays every day. I can.' And I did, to the amazement of both the teachers and pupils. From then on I was hailed as the child musical prodigy, and the attention of two of the teachers of Hull House was called to my gift. One of them interested herself in my behalf and came and called on my mother, asking that she might teach me.

" 'Finally my parents, who were none too rich in worldly goods, and besides there were many brothers and sisters, consented that I take up music even though I was then less than six years old.

" 'For eight years I studied and taught in Hull House and that, I believe, is the most wonderful thing that could have happened to me in the formative period of my life, for I never heard anything except the most classical music from the greatest composers, and I also associated only with the people there who were striving for art in its very highest sense, and who had no time for the artificial or insincere.

" 'My aim is only in one direction and that is to express the true music, the serious compositions of the great master musicians, Beethoven, Mozart, Brahms, Richard Strauss, Schuman, Chopin and others.

" 'It is a rather difficult thing in this day of commercialism to keep always in the atmosphere of real art; there are so many chances to solve the bread and butter question with less work and less art. So far, however, I have tried to associate myself only with those who are serious in their own desires toward the expression of the music which will live forever, and I have taken care of myself for some time, also.

" 'Simplicity and greatness go together. Affectation and music just for effect will not bring the most worthy success. The effect may be more spectacular, but in the end it will prove only a failure.

" 'My work as an accompanist is more or less the way of a school to me, for there is something to be learned every day, and to associate with singers and violinists is in itself a great pleasure, and also very beneficial to the young musician.

" 'Work and serious study are the keynote to an

artistic career — talent of course — but unless one has some talent to begin with there is no reason to adopt music as a profession, or for pleasure.

" 'California? Oh yes, I love California. It is all so wonderful — so grand, so free! I walk and ride about through the mountains and along the ocean and somehow it all seems almost too wonderful, too beautiful. And such a climate! After the dreary cold of Chicago, it is like a paradise of flowers and sunshine. It is an excellent place also for the young musician, and all the time it is growing better and better along musical and artistic lines.

" 'Outside of music, I am studying German and French, for I have discovered that the understanding of other languages is necessary in order to interpret the music of the masters. I am willing to sacrifice almost anything to study and to progress — to reach the point where I can feel that I know music in its highest and most sublime sense.

" 'Sometime I hope to be able to feel that I can interpret the wonderful compositions of the great musicians — then I shall feel that I have not lived in vain and that my talent has not been wasted — but one must live and love and suffer and work.'

"And somehow one left the young student musician, as she is pleased to call herself, with a distinct feeling of having touched an earnest, sympathetic, womanly and artistic nature — the type of young girlhood which will blossom into a wonderful maturity, with a realization of many ideals and many ambitions."

For some promising artists, marriage at this stage and in that day might have ended a brilliant career for the bride. So, it is to the credit of both Blanche and Frank that throughout their years together, while faithfully fulfilling her role as a loving wife, she still was able to excel in a very wonderful way in the world of music — not as a performer, but as a composer.

# 7

## No Greater Duty

Ted Spencer today remembers Uncle Frank for many reasons. But the thing that moves him most is when he recalls his uncle's patriotism.

Specifically, he remembers a time, Ted had just finished his first hitch in the Army, when he went to his uncle for advice about where to go from there as far as his career was concerned.

"What do you want to do?" was Frank Seaver's typical response, using the old technique of logic to help a person arrive at a solution to his own problem.

Ted was undecided, he said, and Frank Seaver then suggested several possibilities.

"He even talked about the advantages of becoming a male secretary as a way for a young man to learn the ropes and get ahead in the business world," Ted remembers.

Ted couldn't work up much enthusiasm. "I didn't always take Uncle Frank's advice," he laughed ruefully recently.

"What about the Army?" Uncle Frank then asked.

Ted was not sure, having the sort of misgivings most young men have at the end of that first tour of duty.

"Then he said," recalls Ted, his voice breaking here, " 'Well, I'll tell you one thing, Ted, there is no greater duty a man can do than serve his country in uniform. Granted, you'll never get rich, but if you serve as a man in uniform there is no greater service you can do for yourself, your country and your God.' "

Ted Spencer returned to civilian life only a few years ago after serving twenty-seven years with distinction in the United States Army.

Earl Spencer also encountered a similar conversation with his uncle, which had a great influence on his future. It was before World War II while Earl was still a student at the University of Southern California and living with the Seavers.

"We're going to get into this war," Frank predicted, some time before most people came to that conclusion. "And you might as well try to get into the cream of the services."

Earl, who had always had a yearning to fly, knew what his uncle meant. But he also knew that at six feet-five and one-half inches, he was too tall.

"Well, there's no harm in trying," Uncle Frank insisted.

They tried and Earl's height was waived and he was admitted to flight officer training in the Army Air Corps. He has been flying ever since, eventually serving as a senior pilot for Hughes Air West Airlines out of San Francisco International Airport.

The advice Frank Seaver gave his nephews did not come about as the result of some untried philosophy of his own. Early in 1917, Lawyer Frank R. Seaver exchanged his civilian title for a military one for the duration of World War I. Because of his High School Cadet leadership, his years in the National Guard and his organizational activities in the Naval Reserves, Frank was virtually a veteran military man when his unit was called to active duty.

Frank Seaver and Blanche Ebert had been married six months when he went off to war.

Frank's duty during World War I was as an officer aboard the *USS Pueblo*, an armored cruiser on Atlantic partol. Among the ship's more interesting ports of call outside the U. S. were tropical Bahai and colorful Rio de Janeiro.

Meanwhile, the girl he left behind stayed for a time with Frank's family in Pomona and later with her people in Chicago.

One day during her anxious wait, Blanche was relaxing on the shady lawn of the Seaver's Pomona home when words and musical notes began to collect in her mind. Turning to her piano a short time later, she began to play and put down the composition on paper. The result was a heart-tugging ballad she titled, "Calling Me Back to You" — inspired, of course, by the absence of her beloved Frank. This, the first of several songs she was to compose over the years, was later made famous by the golden voice of John McCormack.

And her lover did indeed answer that plaintive call of his musical young bride. At the end of the war, by then a lieutenant commander, he was transferred to New York where he was assigned to the naval office in charge of de-mobilizing government-appropriated cargo ships and return-ing them to their owners.

Blanche hurriedly joined him in New York.

As a Navy wife in the big city, Blanche had enough time on her hands to again turn to musical composition. She came up with a special arrangement of *The Battle Hymn of the Republic*, a beautiful demonstration of her own pa-triotism. This arrangement was first sung by Estelle Heartt Dreyfus with the Los Angeles Symphony Orchestra. Then it was played in February, 1919 by the Philadelphia Orches-tra, conducted by Leopold Stokowski, and with baritone Noah Swayne and the Orpheus Club of forty voices per-forming. This program held an extra special attraction for the Seavers because it was a memorial concert in honor of Theodore Roosevelt. Later, back in Los Angeles, the follow-ing interesting little feature appeared in the February 19,

1920, *Herald*, under photographs of a baby and Blanche Seaver, with the headline "Lullaby Dedicated to Baby."

"A lullaby, as a result of the great war!

"Or at least indirectly resultant from it.

"It has been written in honor of a wee baby who will not appreciate the compliment for some years.

"The baby is none other than little 'Billie' Doheny, son of the Edward L. Dohenys, Jr., who spent his first year of life at Point Comfort, where his father was in the service of the government.

"That was last year, and also residing there, her husband doing transport service, was beautiful Mrs. Seaver, wife of Frank Seaver, better known to the music lovers of the world as Blanche Ebert Seaver.

"Mrs. Seaver entertained soldiers and sailors in various encampments, and in her spare time composed music.

"The Dohenys and the composer became great friends both at Point Comfort and Washington, hence the lullaby, dedicated to the youngest scion of the Doheny family.

"It is taken from the old poem, 'Where Do You Come From Baby Dear?' and was sung for the first time in public by Estelle Heartt Dreyfus at her concert at Trinity auditorium."

It was also during their stay in New York during the war years, and their connection with the Dohenys mentioned in the news story, that events occurred which were to dramatically change the direction of the lives of the Seavers. When Blanche and Mrs. Edward L. Doheny met in New York, the latter graciously invited the young fellow Angelenos to spend a weekend with them on the Doheny yacht.

The Seavers accepted, thoroughly enjoyed the outing and soon discovered that their hosts obviously enjoyed the company of their young guests. That invitation led to another and then others, and it was not long before the Seavers learned that the Dohenys had more than a passing interest in them.

As so often happens, a comparatively small incident sparked the interest the Dohenys already had in the young couple and prompted an offer which was to have an important influence on the direction of their lives.

Blanche Seaver remembered, "We were on the Doheny yacht one weekend having fun. I had written a song called 'We'll Shove the Rio Grande Clear Down to Panama' and Frank facetiously said to Mr. Doheny, 'Here's a song that will amuse you.' So Frank sang and I played that song, the words of which are historical about the Panama Canal. Mr. Doheny said, 'Great, I'd like to hear it again.' That actually was what ultimately sent us to Mexico."

After the song, the great oil man, already impressed with the young Navy officer as well as his bride, pointedly asked him when he could get out of the service.

"Any time," Frank replied. "I am in charge of processing release papers. I could put my own release through tomorrow."

"Why not do it?" Doheny challenged, "and come to work for me."

Frank Seaver accepted the challenge. The next day — October 14, 1919 — was his last day of service in the Navy.

It did not take the head of the great Doheny oil empire long to realize he had made a very wise choice indeed in this talented and loyal ex-naval officer.

# 8

## Heading a Company in Mexico

Late in 1892, just a few months before the birth of Frank Roger Seaver in San Jose, there arrived in Los Angeles a man in his late thirties who was soon to make important history in the world of industry.

That man was Edward L. Doheny, and there was not much in his past to suggest that his future looked particularly bright. For years Edward Doheny had been combing the West for gold and silver, and when he put up in a small Los Angeles hotel in 1892, he found himself as far as ever from that pot at the end of the rainbow. But his fortunes were soon to change as he began to take an interest in the "black gold" exploration about the country. He was destined eventually to introduce oil production to Southern California as a major contribution to its ecenomy.

Soon after his arrival in Los Angeles Doheny began to build his future, and his fortune, in oil. By the time he hired Frank Roger Seaver, he owned and controlled a far-flung empire, with Pan American Petroleum and Transport Company as the parent concern listed on the New York Stock Exchange, and several subsidiaries.

Doheny employed Frank Seaver as an attorney and one of his first assignments was to travel to Louisiana to check some titles in a Doheny oil field. This did not take long and in December of 1919, he was back at work in the Los Angeles offices of the company.

The next year Doheny suggested that the Seavers go to Norway to see about some ships that had not been returned after the war. This prospect was especially appealing to Blanche, because of her Norwegian descent. But, alas, thanks to her husband's efficiency and devotion to duty, the trip never materialized. Frank determined the Norwegian negotiations could be handled more quickly and just as satisfactorily in New York and Washington.

It was in 1921 that Doheny asked Seaver to go to Mexico City as an attorney and general representative for his Huasteca Petroleum Company, a division of Pan American Petroleum. This turned into a very eventful, busy and happy, and at one time harrowing, period in the lives of Frank and Blanche.

Frank Seaver reacted to the challenge of the rather hectic conditions in Mexico as though he had trained for that particular role all his life. Of course, he had not, but, as he had always done, he immediately began to prepare himself for the task ahead. He, along with Blanche, first learned the language. He learned the customs and history and traditions and politics of the land and got to know the country's business and civic leaders. It did not hurt his position that his company was the largest single taxpayer to the Mexican Federal government at the time. Blanche still has a photostat of a Huasteca Petroleum Company check, dated October 8, 1922, and made out to the "Tesorero General de la Nacion" in the amount of $3,059,614.52! It was signed by Frank R. Seaver and represented a year's royalty on oil at one dollar a barrel.

Since the Mexican government in those days was in rather shaky condition, financially as well as politically, those taxes were of great importance. On at least one occasion, Frank personally delivered advance taxes in the

## FAMILY ALBUM

Both Seavers were always close to their families. Above, left, Frank and Blanche pose with his parents; above, right, Frank stands between his brothers, Byron D., left, and Homer. At left, Blanche plays the piano for her father, Theodore Ebert.

Blanche, left, and her sister, Lillian, third from right, pose with friends. Below, Frank and Blanche are shown at a family reunion in the old Seaver home in Pomona while on a trip to the States from Mexico.

Above, Frank and Blanche with nieces and nephews. Below, Ted and Earl Spencer, sons of Blanche's sister, Mabel, play with the sons of Arthur Schoenfeld, first secretary of the American Embassy, while visiting their aunt and uncle, at Xochimilco in Mexico City.

The Seavers loved to take their guests traveling in Mexico. Above, Frank feeds their dog, "Cop," scraps from breakfast he cooked for Ted and Earl Spencer out in the country. Below, on a sightseeing tour with Blanche's mother and father.

Above, the Seavers are shown with American Chargé d'Affaires Summerlin (pointing cane) and other embassy and U.S. Naval officers. Below, the Seavers with George Creel, an official in the U.S. Navy Department, and Carlotta Algara, one of the grand ladies of Mexico.

Little street urchins in Mexico City such as these inspired Blanche to want to do something for their welfare. The result was the formation of the *Sociedad Humanitaria de Damas*, a group of Mexico women and women from the American community, who started a home for homeless boys of the street.

form of gold so that the government could meet its army payroll!

Mexico's vast potential, despite the economic and political unrest, represented a challenge for Frank and he moved surely with his great organizational and developmental talents on behalf of his company. He was not long in seeking and getting permission from the home office to develop local markets for their petroleum products, which was an innovation at the time.

With the green light for developing local markets, Frank soon obtained contracts to supply all the fuel oil used by the Mexican National Railways. These were days when fuel oil was used far more extensively than all other petroleum products. Gasoline, on the other hand, had a very low priority in Mexico simply because there were not enough roads for any significant amount of auto travel. A less imaginative man might very well have bypassed gasoline as a marketable item in Mexico. Not Frank Seaver. If lack of roads was the problem, then there was only one way to solve it, Frank reasoned, and that was to build more roads.

Since road building was not the business Frank Seaver was in, he took another course. He went to the Mexican government and convinced the officials to launch a road-paving program. He got a firm which he knew, Burns Brothers of Chicago, to come down to do the paving. It started in Mexico City and fanned out all over the countryside. This opened the way for increased auto sales and use and, of course, a market for Huasteca gasoline.

Significantly, as is often the case with innovative ideas, the road program benefitted the company in other ways, including the creation of outlets for the company's asphalt production in the paving of the roads.

Not long afterward, Frank introduced another American custom to the land south of the border.

When Frank Seaver moved to Mexico, what little gasoline the country marketed had to be purchased in five-gallon cans. Persons fortunate enough (if that is a good choice of words, considering the condition of the roads then) to have autos simply punched a couple of holes in the top of the cans and poured the contents into the auto tanks. Then they returned the cans to the supplier to be used over and over again by soldering the holes in the top. Thus, with better roads opening up new territory to the automobile, Frank decided to do something about the primitive gas-can method of marketing gasoline.

What he did was to start building service stations. His masterpiece, a structurally sound and architecturally appealing service station was located in a *glorietta*, one of the circles along the *Paseo de la Reforma* near Chapultepec Castle. This massive structure had entrances from four directions and a great carved stone arch resembling a famous old Mexican landmark. Then, as the paved roads extended to become highways to other towns, Frank selected other desirable sites, obtained property rights and continued pioneering a chain of service stations.

Frank Seaver's business acumen was not going unnoticed by his employer. During the seven years he headed up the Huasteca operations, he made two important advancements, the first to the title of general manager, and the second to vice-president of the company.

Despite his successes, Frank Seaver changed very little throughout his entire lifetime. Everyone who knew him agrees.

"He was one of the most modest men I ever knew," nephew Ted Spencer recalls. "Even when Earl (Ted's brother) and I were little kids, he always showed us things the company had accomplished as examples of what could be done by man under difficult circumstances. But he didn't do this from the viewpoint of 'look what I built' — he just wanted to show what could be done by working hard and keeping your nose to the grindstone. In all the years I knew him, he never tried to show off his power, money or accomplishments. Uncle Frank — the best way I can describe him — was awe inspiring in a quiet sort of way!"

# 9

## A Humanitarian Project

Frank Roger Seaver had a very interesting philosophy about the relationship of man and woman.

Earl Spencer recalled recently that he had been fussing with his wife one time early in their marriage and went to talk to Uncle Frank about it.

"You want to stay married?" Uncle Frank asked the troubled young husband.

"Yes."

"Then do what she says!" his uncle proposed.

Earl laughs about it now. "It was that simple to him."

Those who knew Frank well know that his philosophy about getting along with a wife in no way reduced his position as head of the house. He simply believed that marriage called for certain concessions from both sides and he never overlooked his own responsibilities in that respect.

"We never had a fight," says Blanche, "though we were both strong-willed. When something would come up, we just never blew up at the same time, and as a result we'd always end up in each other's arms, hugging and kissing. And we were sweethearts to the end."

In the first place, as far as his own wife was concerned, Frank Seaver realized that he had captured a celebrity when he won the heart of Blanche Ebert. But he married her in spite of that fact.

"Uncle Frank never did like his picture in the paper,"

said Earl. "He didn't really like to go to a party, either, although once he was there he enjoyed it because everyone liked him and liked to talk to him."

Added Ted: "But anything Aunt Blanche wanted to do, he was ready. I never heard him say a cross word about going out somewhere. And he was the world's fastest dresser. He'd get home from the office and he'd lie down to read for a while, and Aunt Blanche would be almost ready to go somewhere. Then he'd jump up, shower, get on his tux and be out at the car waiting and calling, 'Come on, Mama'."

Thus their stay in Mexico was a real test of strength of the ties that bound these two unusual persons together. Blanche had earned her position as a musical celebrity so she was immediately pressed into the swirl of social affairs, both in the foreign and Mexican communities, from the outset. Frank, of course, as head of a prominent international firm in a foreign capital, was obligated to also fill a significant role in social and civic activities.

"When we were married," says Blanche, "I fit my life into my husband's life and I never regretted it. I quit concertizing and gave up much of my musical activity because it involved travel, and I wanted only to be with Frank."

But, being a true artist, she never turned her back to her music and it probably was the absence of performing that caused her to turn to composing.

The Seavers moved to Mexico City early in April, 1921, and it was Blanche's determination to give her husband a birthday party which almost immediately involved them in the social world of that great metropolis. They moved into a hotel at first and Frank's birthday, April 12, was fast approaching. Not knowing where else to turn, Blanche went to see the American *charge d'affaires*, a man by the name of Summerlin. It proved to be a wise move because Summerlin readily helped her with a guest list, and told her where she could purchase a decent birthday cake. Later

Summerlin was to become their neighbor when the Seavers moved into a grand old *hacienda* and Doheny donated land across the street upon which the American embassy was built.

During their early years in Mexico, there was no stable government in the country recognized by the United States, and at times the embassy staff was without an ambassador at its head. Consequently, many contacts between the two countries were carried on informally through Frank Seaver's office. But, while international relations were informal, international social relations were very formal indeed, and even when Mexico City was cut off from the outside world — as it was twice during the stay of the Seavers — the international set there still dined in white-tie elegance.

In a huge scrapbook, yellowed and brittle with age, the story of the Seavers' social life is told in news clippings (many in Spanish) and invitations from heads of many foreign states as well as Mexican officialdom, programs of all sorts of grand affairs, and photographs of the Seavers in the company of the most important people in the land. When Jane Addams, the great old friend of Mrs. Seaver's days at Hull House in Chicago, came to visit them, the Mexico City newspapers played it up with much fanfare. When the Dohenys would visit, they, too, received prominent attention from the nation's press. Once Doheny, Seaver and E. R. Jones, president of Wells-Fargo, were caricatured (Blanche calls it "a horrible likeness of Frank — horrible!") in a double-page newspaper spread as "Men About Town." Frank's promotions also caused headlines, as did many other of his business accomplishments.

But the Seavers, despite their heavy social obligations, took a view of their position in Mexico far beyond their formal life as guests and hosts in the community. They believed that as Americans abroad, it was their first duty to become a part of the native community as well as the

American Colony. They made friends with as many Mexicans as they possibly could. To learn the language, they engaged a teacher and Frank took his daily Spanish lesson before breakfast. Blanche took hers following breakfast. Then at night they would read aloud together from a Mexico City newspaper and listen to recordings in Spanish. Soon both were on easy conversational terms with their new Spanish speaking friends and maintained warm relations with many of them through the years.

Their concern did not stop there. They became involved in a unique benevolent project that set the pace for a longtime record of philanthropy that has been excelled by few individuals living anywhere.

They were still living in the hotel in downtown Mexico City when Blanche's attention was drawn to the plight of many homeless children.

"Oh, my, look at that!" she exclaimed to Frank on their first stroll in Mexico City's streets at night.

She was pointing at a recessed doorway of a closed business establishment where several boys were huddled together sleeping on piles of old newspapers. Her dismay increased as they continued their walk and saw that there were many children in the same desperate situation.

"Those are the little merchants of the street you see selling peanuts and tacos everywhere," Frank explained.

He chuckled. "One thing about it, you sure have to admire their spunk!"

"I agree," said Blanche. "But something has to be done about **that**! Oh, my!"

"OK," responded her husband. "Let's do it."

Typically, Blanche tackled the problem head-on. She took it directly to the Mexican people of influence. First she approached her friend, Silvia Conti, a society matron, and convinced her that something needed to be done for the homeless children.

"If we can get Esther interested," Mrs. Conti mused, "we could really do something."

Esther was Esther Ponte, wife of the Mexican secretary.

"Then let's get her interested," Blanche pressed.

Esther Ponte was interested and agreed to lend her name to the movement, which soon developed into the *Sociedad Humanitaria de Damas para Ninos sin Hogar*. Soon many other prominent women, both in the Mexican and foreign communities, were involved and the newspapers were faithfully reporting their fund-raising activities for the homeless children.

Money poured in and it was not long before a home was established with warm beds and good food for eighty-five of the waifs. A program to teach them to read and write was also initiated.

"We didn't have any trouble getting these boys cleaned up and fed," Blanche recalls. "But they absolutely refused to get their hair cut because this was one way they had of getting centavos out of the tourists — 'please, mister, buy my peanuts so I can get a haircut'!"

When Jane Addams, a great philanthropist herself, visited the Seavers in Mexico City she was very much impressed with the program Blanche had started for the homeless boys. Miss Addams and her friend, Mary Smith, stayed a month, and the Seavers took them all over the country. But the great lady expressed her most lasting impression one night at a dinner of the *Sociedad Humanitaria de Damas para Ninos sin Hogar*.

Blanche had been called on to give a report on the program and when she finished Jane Addams turned to her dinner companion.

"Aren't you proud of that girl?" she said.

Frank Seaver grinned. "I sure am," he fervently replied.

# 10

## A Philosophy About the Young

"He was all man. Period."

That is the way Ted Spencer describes his uncle, with a conviction that dates back to the early 1920s when Ted and his brother, as little boys, visited the Seavers in Mexico City.

"He taught us kids to be independent and to stand up on our own hind legs," Ted reflects. "And he also had a keen sense of humor — a dry sort of humor — and he often expressed it in unusual ways."

Like the relationship between the boys and the Seavers' dog, "Cop," a great German shepherd that lived with them in Mexico City.

"He taught us to respect the dog, without fear," Ted recalls. "Then one time he ran a test on us to see if we had gotten the message."

Despite the extremely busy schedule the Seavers had, they managed to get out in the country whenever they could and enjoy the things that God had created. This became a regular thing when the Spencer boys were visiting.

"He liked to start early — he was always a real early bird in whatever he did — and cook pancakes for us out in the wilds," Ted related.

Then that one day he really shook the boys up for a few anxious moments. They had enjoyed a great breakfast and had romped and hiked about the hills. Uncle Frank had tied "Cop" to a tree when they came back to the picnic site. Finally it was time to go home. They packed everything in the car. Uncle Frank started driving away when suddenly both boys started bawling.

"What's the matter, fellows?" he asked.

"Cop!" they cried in unison.

"You forgot Cop!" yelled Earl, the younger of the boys.

"Well, I sure did," Uncle Frank pretended and started turning the car back. "But *you* sure didn't!"

The boys, feeling like great heroes for "saving" the animal, naturally loved the dog more than ever after that. Which is the way Uncle Frank had it figured.

"For a man who never had children of his own, he had a great insight into how to treat kids," Ted says. "He wanted to instill in children the feeling that 'you are worth while — you should *want* to grow up to be a real man, an honest person.' He convinced us we should never lie to get ourselves out of a jam, to take our medicine if we did get into trouble. He was no man to put up with chicanery of any form. He was one of the most honest individuals I ever knew, and I saw it when I was very young."

Frank's interest in the young people in his own family, his wholehearted support of Blanche's work with the young Mexican orphans, and later with her involvement in the Guadalupe Youth Center for Mexican-Americans in Canoga Park, California, reflected what was to be a lifetime of devotion to causes designed to help the young. Because of this deep devotion to youth, Frank and his wife poured literally millions of dollars into similar causes.

"Frank had a very simple philosophy about that," Blanche says. "He loved his country and he always said the only way to keep it from decay from within, strong, and to protect it from threats without, was through education of the youth of the country." When she said that, construction was nearing completion on the ninth major building the Seavers had financed for several educational institutions, to say nothing of countless charities devoted to the health and welfare of the young.

The way the Seaver philosophy was being extended, even during their early years in Mexico City, was reflected in a newspaper account of the inauguration of the house for homeless boys in October of 1923. Their idea even then was to use money to help the young to help themselves. The newspaper described the program:

"The *Sociedad Humanitaria de Damas* may well be proud of what they have accomplished in the nine months' time towards helping the poverty-stricken boys of the streets; for now, instead of sleeping in the streets, they have a clean house and comfortable beds; instead of no food, they have two substantial warm meals daily; instead of ragged clothes, they have clean blue denim overalls for daytime and white cotton sleeping garments for nighttime.

"The children are gradually being taught economy and to save the money which they make in the streets. Although not one single penny is required of them in the home, they have been urged to save their money earned in the streets, in order to buy themselves shoes, and for the reward thereof, they are given new clothes for day and nighttime use.

"The result that the *Sociedad Humanitaria de Damas* hopes to inspire in these boys is: cleanliness, economy and the desire to learn a profession with which they may earn their own livelihoods."

All of which sounds very much like a page from Frank Seaver's own book of life.

# 11

## Enter John McCormack

Mexico City days were bright with music and filled with friendships and good deeds for the Seavers. Blanche was captivated by the music of Mexico.

"But I didn't like the piano with their music, so I learned to play the guitar," she says.

Buffy Kirk, who became the U. S. Ambassador to Mexico and a resident of the embassy home across the street also liked the local music. He would frequently come over for coffee in the morning and join Blanche in singing favorites of the country in the native tongue accompanied by her guitar.

Though it was not easy to find the time, Blanche again turned to musical composition, especially when Frank was away on some of his business junkets to points like Tampico and Vera Cruz.

One thing which inspired her was a prayer Mrs. Doheny sent her one time. It was entitled, "Just for Today," and Mrs. Doheny requested that she set the words to music to be sung at a midnight mass in the Doheny home on the approaching Christmas Eve.

"Lord, for tomorrow and its needs I do not pray;

Keep me, my God, from stain of sin, just for today."

Blanche found the words deeply appealing and she longed to settle down to work on the music to fit the words.

But, in addition to the usual demands upon her time and energy, the prayer came during a period when she was entertaining house guests. Weeks passed and Christmas was rapidly approaching.

One morning she decided she could delay no longer. She sent her house guests out on tour with the chauffeur with instructions not to return until dinner time. She shut herself in her gold *sala*, a necessity for any elegant Mexico City household, and faced her golden piano. At the close of the day, back came the guests demanding news of the progress of the song.

"Not yet," Blanche had to say.

The next day, away went the guests again. This time Blanche was determined to create a musical mood for the job at hand. She got out family mementos, including many of the songs her father loved. Then, suddenly, as she played and sang and drifted along on a flood of memory, she heard the voice of her father (then gone from this world) singing the opening phrases of the prayer. So vivid was this experience that she was able to set down those phrases, melody, accompaniment and all. Once the mood was set, the rest came easily. All morning she worked alone, playing over and over the beautiful and reverent music. After lunch, traditionally siesta time for the servants, there came a knock on the door of the *sala*. When Blanche acknowledged the signal, the door opened and Juana, the Indian cook, entered. Her words touched Blanche.

"Oh, Senora," she said, "what is it that you are playing? *Es muy religiosa, muy bonita!* (very religious, very beautiful)."

But, alas, the house guests did not react the same way, nor, as it turned out, did the music catch on at the Los Angeles mass. This was probably because the arrangement had been set by Blanche for the voice of Estelle Dreyfuss, who became ill a week before Christmas and was unable to perform. The song was sung by an operatic protege of Mrs. Doheny's and it may have been that her voice and delivery simply were not suited to the quiet reverence of the prayer. Whatever the cause, the composition seemed doomed to oblivion until John McCormack entered the scene.

It was some time later, while the Seavers were on a visit back to the States, that they were yachting guests in the same party with that great Irish tenor. Standing with him at the rail at one point on the cruise, Blanche half-jokingly sang him the climactic phrases of her romantic ballad, "Calling Me Back to You."

"Blanche," declared the great singer in his rolling Irish brogue, "if the rest of the song is as good as the climax, you've got a song there. I'd like to see it."

A short time later Blanche stopped by the Ambassador Hotel where McCormack was staying. She was carrying a magazine whose pages contained not only a copy of "Calling Me Back to You," but also the manuscript of "Just for Today," which she had slipped in previously for safe keeping. McCormack immediately took the magazine and began to thumb through the pages.

"What's this?" he asked upon discovering the pages of the manuscript.

"Nothing," Blanche said vaguely, remembering the reception it already had received. Besides, she didn't want to distract his attention from the ballad she had come to show him. But John McCormack would not be put off. He insisted on keeping it for a day or two.

That evening he telephoned Pomona where the Seavers were visiting in the old family home.

"Blanche," he said, "my valet and I have been sitting here like two great fools, blubbering our hearts out over that prayer of yours."

John McCormack was completely sincere about his feelings for the song and he demonstrated it with action. He included that prayer in every program he sang for the next twelve years of his remarkable career. Often his program included "Calling Me Back to You," as well. When McCormack first sang "Just for Today" in Los Angeles in 1927, a reviewer noted how "an immense Shrine Auditorium crowd broke into applause after a moment's inner listening to the message of the song." Thus was justified Blanche Seaver's original feeling about the work and the simple reaction of the first person who ever heard it played, the Indian cook, Juana, when she uttered *"Es muy religiosa, muy bonita!"*

Afterward, in his film, "Song of My Heart," one of the half-dozen songs John McCormack chose to use was "Just for Today." He also made Victor recordings of these two of Blanche's songs. Other great artists such as John Charles Thomas, Ezio Pinza, Bidu Sayao, Madame Schumann Heink, Jerome Hines, Richard Crooks and Igor Gorin have since enriched their concert, radio and television programs with those and others of Blanche Ebert Seaver's compositions.

# 12

## Holdup in Mexico!

The October 18, 1924, edition of *Excelsior*, a Mexico City newspaper, featured the Seavers, including a photograph of the beautiful American matron, in a lengthy page one story.

The story had nothing to do with the world of music, high society, the oil business or philanthropy. Instead, it featured the Seavers as participants in a real live drama, easily the subject of a television series or a Wild West movie.

The story was Blanche Seaver's own account of a hair-raising train robbery, a not uncomman occurrence for that day. The Seavers had been to Chicago for the funeral of Blanche's father and were returning to Mexico City.

At Laredo they boarded Passenger Train No. 4 on Wednesday morning, October 15, and the train headed south. Behind the engine and tender were two express cars, two baggage cars, two second class coaches, a first class coach and the Pullman. The Seavers rode in the Pullman.

Riding in one of the second class coaches were six armed soldiers, who were there for the purpose of guarding a sizable amount of silver in a safe in one of the express cars.

Meanwhile, as the train traveled southward, a band of rebels were busy working on the track below the town of Saltillo. They loosened a section of rail on a trestle at a sharp curve, then waited.

At about 9:45 p.m. the train rounded the curve and the engine hit the loose rail. The engineer made a heroic effort to brake the train, but it was too late. The engine hobbled across the splintering ties, nosed off a slight embankment on the other side of the trestle and overturned. The engineer died in the wreckage. A fireman was fatally injured. The four following cars also went off the track and overturned, and the remainder of the train came to a jarring halt. At that moment the band of outlaws charged out, shouting, "We are Torres' men." Demetrio Torres was a notorious bandit of the day.

The 1924 newspaper romantically described the indident:

"Six swarthy bandits, poorly clad, armed with revolvers, knives glittering in their belts, each carrying a loaded and leveled rifle, prodded and poked half-clad passengers out of their Pullman berths during the holdup of the southbound Laredo train on Wednesday."

The same writer interviewed Blanche in her home three days later and, in her own words gave an account of what followed:

"It was a few minutes before ten o'clock Wednesday night," Mrs. Seaver said. "Many of the passengers had retired, others were in the process of going to bed and the majority of the berths were made down.

"I was at one end of the Pullman, Mr. Seaver had gone to the extreme opposite end when, with a terrible crash, the train came to a sudden halt. I was thrown heavily, but uninjured, against the side of the car. Following the crash, rifle firing began and I should say, lasted about ten or fifteen minutes. It seemed like hours to me.

"I then started back towards the center of the

car and found all the passengers — men and women — stretched out flat on the floor, so I did likewise. I had no idea where Mr. Seaver was. I whistled while on the floor and from the other end he returned the call, to my great relief.

"In this position all of us remained for what seemed like hours, not minutes. I noticed that one of the women took her watch from her wrist and threw it under a berth. From my point of vantage I did the same with a very dear gift of mine which I treasured immensely.

"All of us were in this position when the brakeman came in and called that the rebels had told him to inform the Pullman passengers that they intended to search the car.

"Soon they came, six of them, all armed. They were looking for the conductor. One of them, who seemed to be the only rough one of the lot, in spite of their unkempt appearance, gave the order for all passengers to get off the train. But, to the relief of all of us, another one said that we should remain in the car and he emphasized the fact that we should not leave it, under penalty of death. All were glad to stay. They went away.

"Shortly afterwards they came back again and this time took with them the fire hatchet from its glass case and we heard them later banging at what proved to be the safe from the express car.

"After a long wait they came back, this time accompanied by the brakeman, who was trembling from head to foot, as indeed most of us were. He carried his cap in his hands and with this in front of him was marched down the center of the train, the six armed men with their rifles leveled at him.

"One of them gave the order that we should

throw into the cap all our money and all our valuables, which all the men did, each in turn showing his empty pockets after the men had passed by him. The women in the car gave up their valuables and quite a small fortune was gathered by the holdup men. However, they did not at any time bother any of the hand baggage.

"In the meantime, to our pain and sorrow, the fireman, who was painfully injured, was brought into the Pullman car where some of the passengers helped him all they could and bandaged his right arm, which was badly crushed.

"They then left us and, exactly three hours after the train had been stopped, apparently went away, for nothing but stillness followed from outside. None of us left the pullman, as all decided it was much safer to remain there.

"So far as our trunks were concerned, these were buried in the wreckage of one of the baggage cars and we left them at the spot, but they were not carried away, as apparently the bandits received word that help was coming, and fled to the hills."

It was later determined that several of the second class passengers had been injured in the wreck and that two of the soldiers were fatally wounded in the exchange of gunfire with the outlaws. But the safe proved too strong for the bandits and it was found, scarred, but unopened, when a new unit of soldiers arrived at the holdup scene. Finally a relief train arrived to take the weary passengers on to Mexico City.

It was an experience the Seavers never forgot.

# 13

## In Business for Himself

Frank Seaver had become vice-president of Huasteca Petroleum Company before it was sold to Standard Oil of Indiana in 1925. He continued for nearly two years in that capacity for the new owners, but then began to get the urge to do something on his own. A summary of his feelings about his years in Mexico was contained in this farewell message, as it appeared in *Eonita Huasteca* in September, 1927:

"Having had the fortune to be chosen to take charge of the organization of a new petroleum enterprise in the United States, I am ceasing my active part in the management of the Huasteca Petroleum Company, and I shall not return to Mexico for the present. I hope, however, to continue my personal interest in the progress and activities of the company, ready at any time to give my help and advice to it, if it is thought necessary. I also hope to visit Mexico several times in the future. The organization which I had the pleasure of building, and of which I formed a part, will continue working as it has up to now; I am confident that the useful and cordial relations which exist both within and outside the company will continue unchanged, and that La Huasteca, which has become a familiar name and a real national institution, will continue to give greater and better service to the Republic, to the satisfaction of its inhabitants. I wish to take this opportunity to express my sincere appreciation and thanks to all those who in any way have helped me in the success of the organization which I am now leaving; as well as the Mexican people in general, for the generous and hospitable treatment of which I was the object during my six years of residence in their country. To all those with whom I had the pleasure to come in contact, whether in business or social life, as well as in the government of Mexico, I am happy to send my best wishes and cordial greetings."

The new company Frank referred to in the opening of his farewell message to Huasteca was Pacific Petroleum Products Company, which Doheny had invited him to help organize in Los Angeles. This company was being set up to market some twenty million gallons of gasoline, and build tanks and service stations in the San Francisco area.

Not long after the company was organized, Doheny sold it and this gave Frank the opportunity he had been mulling over in his mind about a business of his own. What he had in mind was the Doheny Stone Drill Company.

Controlled by Doheny's Petroleum Securities Company, it had land, buildings and equipment, mostly in Torrance, and sporadically employed some 50 to 75 people, but had no steady basis of operation. Frank offered to take over the buildings and equipment on a ten-year lease.

"We were having dinner with the Dohenys one night in their Chester Place home," Blanche recalled. "I heard Frank say, 'I'd like to buy the Doheny Stone Drill Company.' Mr. Doheny said, 'You would, Frank? What would you do for money?"

"I've got all the money," Frank replied to the amazement of the great oil man.

Chuckles Blanche, "He didn't know that Frank had been saving his money ever since he was a boy packing oranges in Pomona! He always operated on the theory that a part of every dollar he earned had to be saved!"

Thus it was that in the depths of the Great Depression of the late twenties and early thirties, Frank Roger Seaver took over an almost defunct concern and organized the great Hydril Company, which today is the center of a firmly knit web of factories, products and subsidiary companies. Those first years of industrial operation, of course, demanded perseverance and determination. They ate into the capital laid by as a result of much hard work and frugality. But after the first two years the business was in the black and on its way.

Ted Spencer, with his insight into the character of his uncle, searched for the secret of Frank Seaver's success and concluded, "He was a thinking man, always with something constructive on his mind. He never wasted time, although he didn't bustle around showing outward signs. It always impressed me by the quiet and dignified way he conducted himself and ran his business. He was always the same way."

Blanche remembers her husband as "a walking encyclopedia — a man with an insatiable thirst for knowledge and a mind like a sponge. But once in a while," she laughs, "I'd ask him a question he couldn't answer, and I'd say, 'but you're *supposed* to know'!"

Ted added, "He even used to study a big dictionary! Every minute was precious to this man, and he used every second in some constructive way."

Frank was very modest about his own abilities. "You're the genius, Mama," he used to tell Blanche. "I'm just a plugger."

But this "plugger" was also a genius as a businessman and not the least of the reasons for this was the way he dealt with the people he employed.

Earl Spencer remembers: "I used to work for Uncle Frank during the summers, and half the people who came in to see him just came to talk to him, ask his advice. He was the type who invited great confidence and one who was genuinely interested in other people."

Laughs Ted, "Yes, and by the time you got through a conversation with him, you thought you had figured out your problem by yourself. You could sit down with him and I don't care what subject you'd bring up, he could discuss it intelligently. First he wanted to know all the details and then he'd start asking questions which inevitably led you to figure out for yourself the logical conclusion. It was fantastic, the way he managed it!"

Earl recalls that often Uncle Frank's solutions were so simple that it left others wondering why they hadn't already thought of the answer. He told about one time when Hydril was running three different ads in three trade publications every month. One day one of the officers of the company came to Frank with a handful of advertising copy and complained about the cost of the program.

"Don't those magazines all have different readerships?" Frank asked.

"Yes."

"Then why not run the same ad in all three?" was Frank's simple solution.

No one had thought of that.

Because of Frank's concern for and interest in his employees, he commanded their greatest respect and devotion.

"For instance," said Earl, "I have seen him on the phone talking business to the New York office for half an hour. Then, with the business taken care of, he'd say, 'Well,

George, how's the family?' and ask about each one individually, for another ten minutes. He had the interest of his people at heart and they knew it and were loyal because of it."

Blanche added: "Frank Seaver is *still* the guiding light at our board meetings. When decisions have to be made they are always approached on the basis of 'what would Frank have done?' When Frank was with us, problems used to come up and everyone would get out their slide rules and about the same time someone had it figured out, Frank, who didn't have a slide rule, would give the answer."

It was also during his early years as a budding industrialist that Frank began to heed the advice of his father about investing in land.

Earl Spencer remembers driving "out in the country" one day with his uncle. The country happened to be the location which was to become the expensive Palos Verdes Estates. Uncle Frank got out of the car and walked around, thoughtfully surveying the open fields.

"What are you doing?" the young man asked his uncle.

"Just seeing what kind of potential is here."

"You thinking about buying it?" Earl wondered.

"Well, I might," conceded Uncle Frank.

And he did. He bought more than 200 acres of that land for the taxes owed on it during those depression years and most of it remained in the family until Mrs. Seaver donated it to Pepperdine University to help build Seaver College.

"All you have to do," Frank once told Ted Spencer, "is save a little money, get it in the bank and let it grow. Put away an amount every month, it doesn't matter how much. By and by you will find something you can purchase at a bargain and later sell at a profit. When you sell, put that money in the bank and let it earn interest for you until something else comes along that you can buy at a bargain."

Frank Seaver gave that same kind of advice to his employees. The ones who heeded it found it not only worked for them, but that they received extra rewards from their boss at promotion time.

# 14

## Building a Unique Company

When Frank Seaver took over the Doheny Stone Drill Company in depression days, the salaried employees had been working on half salary off and on for the previous three years.

Cal Drake, a senior vice president and one of the original employees, noted, "When Mr. Seaver first came in we were literally fighting for survival. People who worked for him were glad to be earning a salary and it was in their own interest to help him make a go of the business."

"I didn't even have a salary," recalls Earl Daniels, now senior vice president of Hydril. "I was working on a commission when Mr. Seaver came."

Daniels soon convinced Frank Seaver though that he should put him on a salary. Frank had agreed in a weak moment to pay Daniels a ten per cent commission on the sale of big tools then manufactured by the company.

"Shortly after that I sold a big rig and went in and told Mr. Seaver he owed me $2,800," Daniels remembers with a laugh. "He decided then he'd better give me a regular job."

Cal Drake joined the Stone Drill Company in 1927

right out of high school and was on hand when the new plant in Torrance was built in 1928. He did all sorts of jobs eventually settling in the accounting department as a clerk. He met Frank Seaver when he took over the business as manager for Doheny but it wasn't until a few years later that he really became a close friend. Drake left the company in late 1931 or early 1932 and worked at assorted jobs in the Los Angeles area until called back in early 1935. In the meantime, Frank had become proprietor of the company on August 1, 1933.

"And it *was* a proprietorship," Drake recalls. "Mr. Seaver was a dictator — a benevolent dictator, to be sure — but he ran the show. And when he first took over that company he was a tiger. He had his life's savings on the line and he was determined to make a success of the firm."

Cal Drake returned to the company to work on the sales order desk. Then, when Ed Acheson was transferred to Rochester, Pennsylvania, in early 1937, Drake was appointed head of the sales order department for a year "until they decided to try to make a salesman out of me."

Drake laughs about that now. "I traveled around with Earl Daniels until they finally gave up on me as a salesman."

Which leads to another facet of Frank Seaver's philosophy in dealing with his employees.

"He wouldn't try to get a person to do something he wasn't capable of doing," Drake says. "But he would squeeze every ounce out of a person that he *was* capable of doing."

So Cal Drake returned to the business end of the company after it became obvious to Frank and others concerned that he wasn't cut out to be a salesman. He became treasurer of the company in 1944 and then was given the additional roles of assistant secretary and vice-president. In his position, Cal Drake became closer to Frank Seaver than anyone else in the company and not only was trusted with handling great sums of money but was privy to the innermost workings of the organization.

"In business he was a remarkable man," Drake says. "His business philosophy, methods and policy were, in my opinion, very unconventional. But they worked. He didn't, for instance, believe in debt and that is why we have been so sound all these years where a lot of companies that went into debt are in trouble today. Hydril doesn't have that trouble."

Drake, like so many other loyal Hydril employees, knew his work was pleasing to Frank Seaver not because he went around patting people on the back but in the way he rewarded them with pay raises and promotions and the interest he showed in their personal affairs.

"Frank Seaver didn't immediately warm up to people," Drake says. "It took time — time for him to get to know you — before you began to realize that he had a personal interest in you. He was a tough, rugged boss but he was fair and never dishonest. When he got ready to do something for you he'd never tell you in advance. If you did your job right he would recognize it and, while he might not tell you, you'd know it by the way he treated you. And Mr. Seaver, believe me, didn't want any yes-men around. He could tell if you were honest. He wanted you to speak your mind and then be able to take it if he didn't like what you had to say."

Earl Daniels, whose position in the sales end of the business didn't allow him a day-to-day association with Frank, nevertheless was around him enough for many years to discover a great deal about his amazing personality.

"I told him that day when he offered me the salaried job that I was a salesman and he wasn't, so I felt like I'd be doing well if we could agree fifty per cent of the time," Daniels chuckles.

Frank went along with that and conceded he wasn't

a salesman, adding: "And I don't want to be — that's your job." Of course, they found themselves agreeing somewhat more than fifty per cent of the time, which accounted for Daniel's rise to vice president in charge of sales and finally to senior vice president.

"He treated me more like a son than an employee," Daniels recalls. "He was a very stern man, but I also knew him as a happy, jolly person. I traveled with him a lot and came to respect so many things about him, especially his honesty and integrity."

Daniels said the first time he met Frank he figured out he was a lawyer, from the line of questioning he put to the young man. "Are you married? How many children do you have? Where did you go to school? How long have you worked here? Are you saving your money?"

"Who could save money in those times?" Daniels laughs. "Except maybe Frank Seaver!"

But Daniels *was* impressed with this kind of philosophy and remembers on another occasion when Frank was giving him a little lesson in economics.

"If you want to impress people with how well off you are, don't buy an expensive coat," Frank told him. "You can buy a coat on credit — and everyone knows that. If you want to impress people, wear your savings deposit slip on the lapel of your coat!"

Often Frank Seaver's lessons in economics took a humorous turn. Daniels remembers, "He had an incisive mind and a quick wit. He used to come to my house a lot and was impressed with one of my avocations — cooking or barbecuing. One day he said, 'I wish I could afford to hire you to cook for me, Earl.'"

On another occasion, Daniels was driving into the office after dark when he noticed the lights on a huge Hydril billboard were not on.

Going into the boss's office, he said, "Mr. Seaver, did you know the lights are out on your sign?"

"Yes," Frank replied, "and if you'll quit, we can re-light it."

Daniels laughs now. "I guess my salary and the cost of lighting that sign *were* about the same."

Another thing which always impressed Daniels about his boss was the intensity of his thinking.

"When talking to him you could never feel sure if he was listening or if his mind was on something far away," Daniels said. "Then once in a while he would nod."

Daniels recalls that Bill Whatley, president of an oil company in the same building in which Hydril executives conducted their business, asked him one day, "What's the matter with that boss of yours?"

"I don't know. Why?"

"Well, I see him in the hall and he walks right by me as if he doesn't see me," the oilman said. "And when I see him at meetings and other affairs, he says, 'Glad to meet you, Mr. Whatley'!"

"Well, he's pretty preoccupied a lot of the time," Daniels conceded.

Then he went to Frank's office and told him about the conversation with Whatley.

"He jumped up immediately, jammed that old hat of his on his head and hurried right down and had a real friendly visit with Mr. Whatley," Daniels chuckles.

Daniels, who was a Democrat in those early days "because my father was a Democrat," learned about Frank's political intensity the hard way. He was in Seaver's office one day with two other members of the firm and one of them decided to have a little fun with the young man.

"Who are you voting for in the Senate race, Earl?" he asked him.

"William Gibbs McAdoo!" Daniels said promptly and proudly.

Whereupon, Frank Seaver rose quickly from his chair, leveled a finger like a pistol at Daniels and said, "*That* shows how much *you* know about politics!"

McAdoo, who was the son-in-law of President Wilson, won the race for Senate that year. It was 1932. And it was that same year, as far as Frank was concerned, that the nation experienced its worst political catastrophe in history, the election of Franklin Delano Roosevelt as President of the United States!

Blanche remembers Frank saying, "When that hypocrite defeated our great Herbert Hoover, he not only upset our country, he upset the whole world."

Frank's foresight in business and investment matters also made an impression on Earl Daniels. "One of the first things he did after taking over the company was to open a plant in Houston to be nearer the oil fields. He bought so much land to go with it that it seemed a waste of money at the time."

Mrs. Seaver corroborates her husband's foresight. "After Frank's death I went to visit the Houston plant and the superintendent took me out to show me the land Frank had bought. When he bought it, they thought he was crazy. Now every inch of it is in use and we wish we had more. But the land is so terribly expensive around there now, we couldn't afford it if it were available."

Then, in 1937, Daniels made a trip to Rochester, Pennsylvania, to look over a huge plant Frank had bought for manufacturing Hydril products.

"It has *one* machine in the whole place," Daniels reported to his boss upon his return to the home office. "It looks like a pea in that big old place."

"Oh, well," Frank responded. "We'll fill it up someday."

"Someday" came in 1941, when the place was filled with

machinery, as Hydril went into full-scale production of war materials after Pearl Harbor.

Cal Drake became involved in that operation, again as a result of Frank Seaver's foresight. It was in mid-1939 when Mr. Seaver decided to open an office in New York and sent Drake to make the arrangements in the East. But his orders were to stop off in Rochester for a month to relieve Ed Acheson, who was due to take a month's vacation. During that month, Hitler invaded Poland.

"Mr. Seaver saw the handwriting on the wall and decided not to open the New York office," Drake says. "And I stayed on at the Rochester plant for the next five years."

Frank's faith in taking over the business during the Depression was rewarded handsomely after the initial lean years. By 1938, Hydril was firmly enough established to enable Mr. Seaver to purchase the land on which the plant was located in Lomita. Then after the war started the government announced it wanted to buy the plant to manufacture engines for ships, and Hydril had to find a new location quickly.

"We found an old plant at Vignes and North Main in Los Angeles and with the help of a Negro and a Mexican carpenter built a couple of more buildings, which are still there. We moved in the spring of 1943," Daniels recalled. "It was a hectic move, not only because we had to get moved in a hurry, but the grounds were one big mudhole and we really had a time moving that machinery. But we finally made it and we are still there. The plant has been adequate for our needs, although we have had to expand our plants nearer the oil fields."

When Frank took over Doheny Stone Drilling Company (the name came from the founder of the business, Fred) Stone), it was manufacturing heavy oil drilling machinery as well as blowout preventers and threads for oil piping. Frank decided to abandon the heavy production and concentrate on the specialty items, the threads and blowout preventers. One contract which gave the young company a great boost came in 1937 when Youngstown Steel Casing decided to put the Hydril threads on its pipe. This resulted in extensive production of that item for Youngstown for many years.

Today the company produces thousands of parts used in oil field equipment, about eighty-five per cent of which are covered by company patents. Leading the line is the Hydril Blowout Preventer, which, as the company catalog proclaims, "takes the 'blow' out of blowouts."

"There's nothing unique about it," Frank used to say. "Every oil man is determined to prevent a blowout and fire. Everybody in the business makes a blowout preventer. But it happens that in every oil field in the world you will find Hydril Blowout Preventers. Normally, unless a very hot fire warps it, a blowout preventer will last many years. Of course, we keep changing and developing our products. In our Los Angeles plant, we can high test our high-pressure items — surge chambers and so on — up to 23,000 pounds per square inch. That's a lot of pressure!"

Of course it didn't just "happen" that the name Hydril excelled all others in the blowout prevention line. It simply is such a rugged piece of machinery that it far outlasts any competitive product. This very fact in itself brought about a change in marketing when it became obvious that the company was working itself out of business by building such good equipment that it rarely needed replacement.

"So what we did," Blanche said, "was start leasing the preventer, instead of selling it. That was Richard Seaver's idea."

Although trained as an attorney and concerned for many years in business affairs, Frank always was intrigued by engineering. He devoted much time to the drawing board and to designing things. Though he had no formal engineering training, his capacity for absorbing information, for cataloging, organizing, retaining it in his mind, plus a natural mechanical aptitude, helped to make him very active in the inventing, designing and manufacturing operations of the company.

Under his skilled guidance and leadership, and through his long hours at the office and in the plants, Hydril grew spectacularly. Shortly after the plant was opened in Rochester, Pennsylvania, in 1938, it became the largest of the Hydril plants. In 1940, Hydril Company of Texas was organized and it operated during the war as Texord Manufacturing Company, producing military ordnance.

During the war, Hydril produced 4.2 mortar shells as well as miscellaneous parts for larger Naval shells. But "Mr. Seaver didn't like to do business with the government," Cal Drake says. "He had no choice during the war and, of course, he felt he was helping the war effort. But as soon as the war was over we got out of government business. Another thing about Frank Seaver and the government was that he didn't take advantage of equipment and land deals that he could have made. So we didn't make a lot of money during the war — he always stressed that we quote a price that would give a fair profit and that's all — because he refused to work all the angles on getting land and equipment from the government."

Some manufacturing is now done in two Canadian locations, one Eastern and one Western. Catchy compound names — such as "Texord" for Texas Ordnance — represent Frank Seaver's attraction to word invention. These names are found throughout the Seaver operation. Some of the other companies he named are Delvermendo, Dranox, Hydraver, Hydril itself, Lasekan, Pendergola and Senox.

Frank was in his glory when he was able to serve his country in time of emergency. He was also devoted to military men when it was time to employ them at Hydril.

"He liked ex-Navy people particularly, especially those who had served on board ship, and no other reference was needed for them to go to work for Frank Seaver," says Daniels.

In 1946, the war over and with steel rationing and oil drilling limitations ended, Hydril resumed its leading peacetime position in oil field equipment manufacture. Business boomed and in seven years business had doubled.

"Frank Seaver was a veritable walking encyclopedia when it came to the oil industry and a lot of other things," says Earl Daniels. "He knew the great oil men of the world. He knew all about such things as the Teapot Dome scandals and other historic events. He knew so many great people socially, too.

"We have an organization called the Petroleum Production Pioneers and a few years before his death, Mr. Seaver was made a lifetime member. One of the things we try to do is get old timers to sit down and review their lives for the association. But we never could get Mr. Seaver to go up there and do it. He was very modest about his own exploits."

# 15

## Grooming an Heir Apparent

Richard C. Seaver didn't know it at the time but his uncle apparently picked him as his potential successor at Hydril before he was, as the old saying goes, scarcely dry behind the ears. Moreover, had not Richard Seaver been of the kind of fiber his uncle thought he was made of, the young man could never have survived the kind of apprenticeship demanded of him.

As might be expected, Hydril was a one-man operation during Frank Seaver's lifetime. He set the policies. He made the decisions. He ran the show.

"This allowed him to move quickly or slowly or however he wanted to move in business matters," says Richard Seaver. "This was significant because the most important thing to him was quality. Sometimes this was hard on people who worked for him. I rewrote legal documents over and over before they would suit him. Letters, bills, air conditioning — everything — had to be quality.

"The next most important thing in business to Frank Seaver was simplicity. He didn't believe in frills of any kind. This was true in products. If someone came up with a complicated product, he'd stall or just say 'forget it.'"

In the selection of his successor, Frank was also concerned with quality and he used the simple approach. That he did not bother to advise the subject of this part of his design for the future of Hydril was obviously part of the design itself. That things worked out as he anticipated is a classic example of Mr. Seaver's planning ability and his understanding of human nature.

Frank Roger Seaver had no children of his own to take over the reins of Hydril. The most logical choice among his blood relatives was the son of Byron Dick Seaver, with whom Frank had practiced law and who kept the name of his brother Frank on the door of his law office until his own death in 1954. Enhancing the attributes of Byron Dick's son was the fact that the young man was a lawyer.

How he got to be a lawyer did not escape Frank's attention. In some ways, it was reminiscent of his own experiences.

Richard Carlton Seaver was born in Los Angeles in 1922 at Good Samaritan Hospital, of which "by an odd coincidence" he is now a trustee. He attended public schools, graduated from Fairfax High and then, in keeping with the family tradition, entered Pomona College. Like his Uncle Frank, Richard became interested in the military and joined the ROTC program at Pomona. When the nation entered World War II, he received his commission as a second lieutenant and went on active duty with the Army Infantry for the duration. After serving in Australia, New Guinea and the Philippine Islands, he was released in January, 1946, with the rank of captain.

Two other events took place almost simultaneously with his release from the Army — his marriage and his return to classes at Pomona.

He laughs now, "I had to make up for lost time."

After receiving his bachelor's degree at Pomona, Richard enrolled in the Law School of the University of California at Berkeley and was graduated in 1950. Within weeks, he was elected secretary and a director of Hydril Company. But it was a long time before the young attorney was to become a full time member of the administration of the organization. If it indeed *was* a marriage made in heaven, the courtship was a long and sometimes rocky one.

In retrospect, the relationship between the two Seavers portrays some of the earmarks of a fascinating chess game.

When Richard received his law degree, he joined Thelan, Marrin, Johnson and Bridges, a respected San Francisco firm of barristers, and was sent to head up their Los Angeles office. Frank promptly opened his game by hiring the firm to represent Hydril. Thus, Hydril had a new director, secretary and legal counsel, all in one man. This arrangement lasted from 1950 to 1957, and it gave Richard seven years of a lawyer-client relationship with his uncle. Frank made sure that he had *every* opportunity to get involved and learn the ropes.

It wasn't until 1953 that Frank Seaver tentatively slid out his next pawn to challenge his legal representative. He did this by dropping the suggestion that as long as Richard was already so much involved with Hydril affairs, he might as well join the company as a salaried employee. Richard, whose salary already was nothing to be sneezed at and whose future looked adequately promising and independent, declined.

"He didn't press me," Richard recalls, "or make any kind of issue about it. But he kept bringing it up from time to time. And I kept turning him down. For one thing, I felt I was worth more money than he was inclined to pay me. If I went to work for him I knew he would fix my salary; whereas, as an attorney, I would set my own limits."

Frank Seaver patiently and carefully moved the pieces, another pawn, a knight, a bishop. Write this. Rewrite this. Look into this. Check that. How about this contract? This pension plan? Is this company a good credit risk? Why don't you come with Hydril?

Business boomed. They took trips together to other

plants. It was a fascinating world, this world of big industry. It was the kind of world of which most young attorneys dream of being a part.

Finally, in 1957, Frank Seaver put his nephew in check with an offer.

"This time I sat myself down and really gave it serious consideration," says Richard. "I got to thinking that if he was not my uncle I would have leaped at the opportunity. So I decided I shouldn't let that prejudice me toward the job. I accepted."

Richard Seaver's duties didn't change appreciably. There just got to be more of them under the new arrangement. He wasn't thinking of some day becoming president of the company, probably because Frank didn't give him a whole lot of time to dream. If Frank was thinking along those lines, he failed to take his nephew into his confidence.

But in all other affairs of Hydril, Frank Seaver *did* take the young man into his confidence.

"I did almost everything," Richard recalls. "I accompanied him nearly everywhere business took him. I did all the legal matters — pension plan, contracts and so on. A lot of people tried to buy Hydril in those days and I sat in on all those discussions. I wrote my own resignation once a month — but, of course, I never turned one in!"

Richard Seaver's statement that he accompanied his uncle everywhere that "business" took him had a very special significance in this grooming of a president unaware.

"Uncle Frank believed in keeping everything departmentalized," Richard explains. "He kept people in one department from knowing what was going on in another unless it was necessary to their function. He kept people from one plant from knowing people at another. He kept me from mixing in his social affairs."

Initially, Richard didn't understand or particularly appreciate that policy. He used to pick up a newspaper and read on the society pages about an elegant banquet or ball the Seavers had hosted the night before and which had been attended by all sorts of prominent and interesting people. Also attending, Richard couldn't help but notice, would be some of his contemporaries, which didn't help his feeling of being left out.

"Then one day he told me why," Richard relates. "He said he had often seen young men become involved in social affairs to the extent that this became their way of life and their careers suffered and often collapsed. Now I can fully appreciate what he meant and I'm thankful he was wise enough to keep me from becoming involved."

In November, 1964, a month after the death of Frank Roger Seaver, the Board of Directors of Hydril Company elected Richard Carlton Seaver as its second president. He was 42 years of age.

As president of Hydril, Richard pursued the philosophy and objectives of the man who founded this remarkable company. His handsomely appointed office is separated by a walk-through closet from a larger office from which Frank Seaver directed the business for so many years. The larger office is much like Frank left it, except some of his honors, degrees and citations now adorn the panelled walls.

"But it is not a shrine to Frank Seaver," Richard says of the big office. "We still use it for board meetings. I wouldn't feel right in using that office for my own because it belonged to the man who established this business. Even today, you see, a great deal of the momentum we have is due to the way he established the business and I can't say that today any of us are responsible for Hydril being what it is. Our role is to guide the things he created."

Richard C. Seaver today finds himself in pretty much the same situation his predecessor occupied, a man departmentalized.

One department is Hydril. Business is such that he finds himself as busy, if not busier, than he was during the days his quality-demanding boss handed him back letters and briefs and contracts to polish and bring to perfection.

Another department is the philanthropy legacy Frank Seaver left. Through the Seaver Foundation, "Aunt Blanche decides who gets the gift, and I handle the money."

The third department is the social obligation which his prestige as head of a major industrial firm requires. Richard grins ruefully. "I like it," he says, "but I do have to be selective. And now I sometimes wonder why I ever became miffed when Uncle Frank left me out of this part of his life!"

Then there is a fourth department that Frank Seaver was never able to enjoy, but one which there is no doubt he appreciated — the role of being a father to five handsome children. They are Richard Carlton II, Christopher, Patrick, Victoria, and Martha.

This is an area of a man's life that would have the wholehearted blessing of Frank Roger Seaver. He once told nephew Ted Spencer, "When you bring children into this world, it is your responsibility to bring these kids up to be honest, God-fearing, upright citizens. That's the greatest thing a parent can do. If you can do that, you've done as much as any parent can do."

Richard Seaver is trying in all departments to carry out the wishes of the man he succeeded as president of Hydril. "You know," he says with a grin, "I'm even accused once in a while of acting like Frank Seaver!"

# 16

## The Chester Place Home

It was in 1930, not long after the Seavers returned to Los Angeles from Mexico, that the Dohenys invited them to occupy the beautiful home at Twenty Chester Place in which Mrs. Seaver still lives in a quiet, shaded residential park.

Since the death of the Dohenys, the entire park has become the property of the Catholic Church and much of it is now a part of the campus of Mount St. Mary's College. But Cardinal McIntyre asked the Seavers to continue to reside there as long as they wished.

The spacious and comfortable Chester Place home reflects the wide-spread interests of the couple who lived there so long together. The concert grand piano holds Mrs. Seaver's two dozen published songs. Scattered about the wide, friendly rooms are photographs depicting a long lifetime of friendships ranging through many lands, from royalty and nobility through leaders of industry and the worlds of music and the arts and public service.

Chester Place was ideal for Frank Seaver. It was within walking distance of his office and he often hiked the couple of miles at a brisk pace.

"The thought of living in suburbia," says nephew Ted Spencer, "was to Uncle Frank the greatest waste of time and money in the world. He was always after his employees to live closer to their work."

It wasn't long after they moved to Chester Place that

"Cubby" came to live with the Seavers, and it was a situation that nobody really planned.

"Cubby" was a dog, a pet that entered the family circle one day in Chicago when a woman walked up to Earl Spencer on the street, pressed the little ball of fur into his hands and said, "You want this doggie?"

Naturally, Earl did. He took him home to his apartment and it wasn't long before it became apparent that Cubby had a way about him.

Almost immediately, the manager of the apartment complained to Earl's mother: "We don't like dogs around here." Mrs. Spencer, now Mrs. Mabel Marks, retorted: "I don't like the silverfish around here, either!"

A week later she observed that Cubby was tagging at the heels of the apartment house manager everywhere he went.

"They were inseparable," Mrs. Marks recalls.

Then Cubby came to California one time with Earl and stayed, since the animal was a comfort to Mrs. Seaver's mother during her invalid years in the Seaver home.

Blanche was talking to Frank one day about keeping the dog.

Frank wasn't exactly sold. "You're going to get dog hair all over everything," he said, and then washed his hands of the matter.

"A month later," Blanche laughs, "I went in the bedroom one evening and there was Frank asleep on one pillow and Cubby on the other."

The dog lived to the ripe old dog age of seventeen, and when it was finally agreed that the ailing animal had to be relieved of his misery, it became a major crisis in the household. Blanche refused to be a party to the act, and it fell Mrs. Marks' lot to hold the dog in her arms while the veterinarian put the poor old fellow to sleep. Everyone, including Frank, was touched with the little funeral they had for Cubby. The Spanish maid was so upset she chastised the others most severely and then refused to speak to anyone for several days.

"I never *dreamed* we'd ever have such a situation over a dog," Blanche tells it now, her eyes misting.

While Frank went forth from the house on Chester Place each day to run the great Hydril Company, Blanche started immediately upon their return from Mexico to become involved in many charitable, cultural and civic affairs.

Among the first groups she became actively identified with was the Nine O'Clock Players (Children's Theatre Guild) and Las Madrinas, a group of matrons who provide financial assistance to the Children's Hospital Convalescent Home. While a member of the Board of Las Madrinas, Blanche was sponsored by Kate Page Crutcher to membership on the Board of Hospitals, a group which she still actively serves.

With her interest and devotion to music, Blanche soon became active in the work of the Los Angeles Symphony Association. She has served on both the Board of Trustees and the Advisory Board for a number of years, and for four years as Program Chairman for the Women's Committee on Symphony Salons. A member of the Symphony Opera Patroness Committee since its inception, she was Chairman of the Sponsoring Opera Patronesses in 1951. The Hollywood Bowl Patroness Committee also has received the benefit of her efforts on behalf of the cultural life of the city.

Always close to the heart of Blanche Seaver has been the health and welfare of children. In 1947, she and seven other women organized the St. John's Hospital Guild to help raise funds for the construction of a seven-floor wing, giving the hospital 118 rooms and three floors of nurseries, including a floor for pediatric care. Later she was one of the twelve women who formed the Los Angeles Orphanage

Guild, first initiated in 1856 by the Daughters of Charity, the oldest charity in Los Angeles. To replace the old Boyle Heights building, which had to be demolished, funds were raised for an orphanage in South San Gabriel where 168 orphans are now housed at "Maryvale."

Blanche is also active on the Board of St. Vincent's Hospital Auxiliary. She has long been an Advisory Board member of St. Elizabeth Day Nursery, which cares for children whose mothers work; the Social Auxiliary, and St. Anne's Hospital Guild. Since 1958, she has served on the Board of Trustees of Achievement Rewards for College Scientists Foundation.

All of this busy and useful life culminated in a distinction which comes to few women, election to the Board of Trustees of a great university. In June, 1960, she was elected to the board of the University of Southern California, the third woman in the history of USC to sit as a member of the board, and the first woman to be so honored in twenty-five years. After Frank Seaver's death, the Board of Trustees of Pomona College, on which Frank had served with distinction since 1947, elected her to its membership. In 1968, she was named a member of the President's Board of Pepperdine College, which had earlier conferred upon her the honorary doctor of fine arts degree. Pomona College gave her an honorary doctorate degree in the fall of 1970.

In 1976, following the 1975 birth of the Frank Roger Seaver College of Pepperdine University, she became a member of the newly reorganized Board of Regents of Pepperdine.

Thus the great old house on Chester Place has been the base of a remarkable schedule of worthwhile activities for Blanche and Frank Seaver for the thirty-four eventful years they lived there together, and for Blanche in the years since his death.

About a year before his death, Frank was not feeling too well and it bothered him greatly that his ailment was slowing him down.

"Mama," he said one day, "I'm going to have to start getting to the office earlier. I'm always the last one in these days."

"Well, that's just too bad," Blanche came back. "You'll just have to keep being the last one in."

What Frank Seaver meant by being the last one there was his arrival at 9 to 9:15, even when he was sick.

The passing of Frank Seaver only heightened Blanche's own activities.

"I have to carry on for both of us now — there were so many things Frank still wanted to get done," she says earnestly.

# 17

## An Amazing Philanthropic Record

Frank Seaver gave away millions of dollars to education and other causes and he always made the gift with one admonition: "Get this money in the bank *today* because you don't want to lose one day's interest."

When his widow made their second donation of $1,200,000 to the University of Southern California, she was keenly aware not only of her late husband's philosophy about giving to independent education, but about his concern for immediate interest.

She accordingly handed the check to USC's President, Dr. Norman Topping, with the familiar words: "Get this in the bank *today!*"

"Well, we want to get pictures first," the educator suggested.

"All right, get on your horse, but get it in the bank *today*," Mrs. Seaver insisted.

Frank Seaver began his philanthropy as a young man when he named Pomona College as the beneficiary of his first life insurance policy. With that beginning he supported many humanitarian causes over the years, homeless children, hospitals, churches, schools.

"He was generous all his life," says Richard Seaver, "but in a relatively modest way until 1956 when he gave away his first million dollars in a single gift."

Again, his Alma Mater was the beneficiary. In the 1968 biography of Rudolph James Wig, fellow trustee of Pomona College, author Clifford M. Drury recounts the gift. Shortly after Wig became President of Pomona's Board of Trustees in 1948, he became aware of the urgent need for a new science building. Wig found fellow board member Frank Seaver equally concerned and they both agreed that a third Trustee, William Johnson, might be the most likely prospect to finance the building. As it turned out, Wig did find Johnson interested, but, alas, before plans for his participation could be culminated, William Johnson died of a heart attack.

Seaver had become so much interested in the projected new building that he gave $50,000 to cover the first cost of detailed plans. When they were submitted for bid the lowest came in at approximately one million dollars.

Wig took the bid to Seaver who told them to proceed and he would donate the full amount.

Says Richard Seaver: "Uncle Frank learned something from that. He learned that it was painless. He had always been conscious of the difficulty of accumulating wealth. But when he gave that money, he discovered that the ceiling didn't cave in on him and the business didn't collapse. On the other side of the fence, he was exposed suddenly to the same kind of people he remembered and had always admired from his college days at Pomona. This was inspiring to him. He had a feeling of accomplishment that he'd never had before. He became a different figure than he'd ever been before. He knew the appreciation was genuine and he liked it. That was a big turning point in his life and from then on his company — his institution — gave away more than a million dollars a year."

The more Frank did the more it inspired him to do, and just as significant, the more it inspired him to persuade others to give.

Richard Seaver tells about one time when Frank and Fritz Burns, another regent of Loyola University, were discussing a need for funds during a break in a board meeting.

"If you'll give $50,000 I will," Frank challenged.

"Okay," readily agreed Burns.

Back in the board meeting, they announced their decision, "and pretty soon, others followed and they had what they needed right there in that room," says Richard Seaver.

"The point is," he added, "he did that without being commissioned to do it."

After making the huge donation to Pomona in 1956, Richard recalls his uncle "worked as hard on that building as he did at Hydril. He made sure they got the best. He was as much a perfectionist there as he was at Hydril. He would go out and look over the construction and if something looked flimsy, he'd say, 'Why is that flimsy?' As a result, that building is top quality. It even has a reinforced concrete roof and will probably outlast the pyramids!"

Frank's awareness of the needs at Pomona did not come about casually. He had served as president of the Alumni Association in 1910 and was in close touch throughout the years. He was elected to the Board of Trustees in 1947 and served in that capacity until his death. The role represented more than a title to Mr. Seaver. He always served as an articulate spokesman for his strong views on the real purpose and goals of a private college, the proper assumption of responsibility by its trustees and the necessity of avoiding unconscious imitation of institutions with lesser or divergent objectives. He also was an active leader in programs for the advancement of the college, contributing in the most positive ways.

Frank's gift in 1956 to Pomona was to finance construction of a magnificent new mathematics, physics and astronomy laboratory and classroom building. As an example of the high goals which he set for his own operations, he informed the faculty of these departments that he wanted no equipment to go into the building that was not equal to the best of any college in America, and his specification was complied with. In addition, he made provision to bring the libraries in these fields up to the same standard. Naturally, professors in those departments still have a very high regard for Frank Seaver!

When the building was completed in 1958, the equipment and furnishings, which bore the pleasant stamp of Mrs. Seaver's discriminating taste and attention to detail, were the best and most advanced available. It was Frank Seaver's request that this building be named for his long time friend, the Nobel Prize winning scientist and developer of the California Institute of Technology, Robert Andrews Millikan.

In 1957, on behalf of his institute, Frank presented another donation to Pomona College for the construction and equipping of a second new science building, this one for the departments of biology and geology. Several months before his death, he made provision for the erection of still another science building — for chemistry — which was dedicated on January 19, 1965.

Mrs. Seaver remembered that Dr. Nelson Smith, chairman of the chemistry library at Pomona, was the person who actually inspired Frank to give the third science building. "He came to Frank's office time after time seeking help and advice for what to do about the old building to bring it up to date," Blanche recalled. "Frank was impressed with Dr. Smith and his devotion and dedication to science and students and the long hours he worked on their behalf. Finally Frank told him, 'You deserve a new building and I am giving you a new building.' And he did."

These three structures, known as the Seaver Science Center, provide facilities for education in the basic sciences in superbly equipped laboratories and lecture rooms, among the finest in the nation. These three buildings and other gifts from the Seavers are a combined investment of well over $7,500,000 and represent the largest that Pomona College has ever received from any individual or family.

It was over Frank Seaver's objections that the Pomona board decided to name the second building the Seaver Laboratory. He adamantly refused the use of his full name on the building and finally reluctantly agreed to assign his last name as an honor to the Seaver family and its long devotion to the college and the town.

On October 16, 1958, the honorary degree of Doctor of Laws was awarded to Frank Seaver by Pomona College. President E. Wilson Lyon said: "Frank Roger Seaver — affectionate son of this valley, distinguished businessman and industrialist, loyal and ever helpful alumnus of Pomona — it is my pleasure by authority vested in me by the Board of Trustees to confer on you the Honorary Degree of Doctor of Laws of Pomona College, with all the rights and privileges appertaining thereto."

The following year, on June 14, 1959, Loyola University also awarded him the honorary degree of Doctor of Laws. The citation read:

"In keeping with its policy of recognizing eminent merit and rewarding illustrious service with academic distinction, Loyola University is privileged this day to single out one worthy of any honor it can confer. Training in science at Pomona College and in law at Harvard, this Native Son of California started on the high road to rich achievement, fortified in the knowledge that the laws of happiness are the laws of service.

"Answering the Call to the Colors in the first World War, he wore the Navy Blue, serving in the Atlantic until his separation as Lieutenant Commander in October, 1919. This experience did much to engender in him a love of the sea and proud he is that to this day he qualifies for that sturdy race of men that go down to the sea in ships.

"Returning to the paths of peace, Mexico was the locale for his genius in organization and leadership for seven years, while directing the vast empire of American interests in petroleum development.

"To an administrative competence of the first order, he brings a creative ability that is responsible for numerous devices and techniques now considered essential to industry. A member of the Board of Freeholders, which drafted the Los Angeles Charter in 1912, his constancy and vigilance in civic affairs have continued throughout the years.

"Patron of Arts and Science, Letters and Philosophy, he has dedicated much of his time and energy to the cause of privately supported education. His benefactions in this and allied areas have been bountiful, always unostentatious and not infrequently anonymous.

"Loyola University is this day privileged to recognize this stalwart Christian gentleman and because of his all-season devotion to the cause of education, as reflected in the independent college, is particularly gratified to present for the degree of Doctor of Laws, Frank Roger Seaver."

On December 6, 1958, the two great buildings at Pomona College — the Robert Andrews Millikan Laboratory and the Seaver Laboratory — were dedicated in a colorful double ceremony on the campus, attended by many friends and associates both of Dr. Millikan and Frank Seaver. The eloquent and impressive convocation address was given by Dr. Detlev Bronk, president of the Rockefeller Institute.

For this occasion Frank Seaver allowed the crossing of departmental boundaries of his life.

"I talked him into inviting people from Hydril to the ceremony," says Richard Seaver. "He was glad he did because our people enjoyed it so much and were proud to see him honored for the things he had done for the college."

Among other major gifts, Frank Seaver donated $750,000 toward the construction of the von KleinSmid Center for international and Public Affairs at the University of Southern California. Von KleinSmid, his good friend and neighbor, was Chancellor at USC at the time of his death. After Mr. Seaver's death, his widow donated another $1,200,000 for a building at USC. Another substantial gift to the First Congregational Church, of which he was a member and a Trustee, was used to build the Seaver Building of Pilgrim School. Mrs. Seaver has since provided a building at Harvard School for Boys in the San Fernando Valley, and a building at Freedoms Foundation, in Valley Forge, Pennsylvania.

"When he left us," Blanche said, "he had completed seven of eleven great buildings he wanted to build. I completed the other four. When I saw that I was free to complete a building on my own, I gave one to Freedoms Foundation at Valley Forge in memory of our Number One American, General of the Army Douglas McArthur, who had been Frank's idol through the years. Although they had only met once, there was a great meeting of the mind and sharing of a mutual philosophy between Frank and General McArthur. I also felt, and knew Frank shared the feeling, that Freedoms Foundation was doing a great work for our country, especially in the Americanism Education program for teachers."

It was significant that in 1970, Mrs. Seaver, who has been on the Board of Freedoms Foundation for many years, asked the young president of Pepperdine University, Dr.

William S. Banowsky, to be the speaker at the dedication of the General McArthur building at Valley Forge.

In addition to serving on the Board of Trustees at Pomona and the Board of Regents for Loyola, Frank Seaver was a trustee and member of the Advisory Board of Mount St. Mary's College and at one time was a member of the American Petroleum Institute, National Metal Trades Association, Petroleum Production Pioneers, the California and Los Angeles County Bar Associations, Harvard Law School Association, Los Angeles Chamber of Commerce, Kappa Delta Fraternity, the American Legion, the Masonic Lodge, Confrerie des Chevaliers du Tastevin, the Wildlife Society, and the Lincoln, Harvard, University, Wilshire and California Clubs of Los Angeles.

Frank Seaver became interested in Pepperdine College in the early 1960s. He was particularly interested in several programs sponsored by the College which he believed uniquely served the American way of life. He was especially interested in the Pat Boone—U.S.A. program, a nationwide radio series heralding the advantages of a system of free enterprise, a series of educational films which the college produced on the subject of Communism, and in the annual Pepperdine Forum, which brought together outstanding intellectual, business, and educational leaders to discuss problems of national and international scope having to do with the welfare of the nation.

One of the early contacts which then Pepperdine President, M. Norvel Young, made with Frank Seaver was through a mutual friend, Henry Salvatori, a long time member of the Pepperdine advisory university board. Salvatori informed Mr. Seaver of the Pat Boone—U.S.A. program and Mr. Seaver responded immediately and generously by sending a gift to Dr. Young to put the program on national radio.

A short time later, in 1961, Frank Seaver attended a

Pepperdine College Forum luncheon at the Biltmore Hotel in Los Angeles which featured his friend, Senator Barry Goldwater, as its speaker. Mr. Seaver not only was impressed by the courageous speech of the Senator from Arizona, but by the overflow audience attracted to the Pepperdine function in the Biltmore Bowl. This prompted a continuing personal and financial interest in later Forums and in other prominent speakers brought to Los Angeles from all over the country.

Typical of Frank Seaver's willingness to help the worthy programs of Pepperdine College was a project which grew out of a conversation during the annual Forest Lawn Writing Awards banquet, a gala event sponsored by the late Hubert Eaton, a personal friend of Frank Seaver. Pepperdine students had won many laurels over the years in the Forest Lawn writing contest, and this year was no exception. The speaker for the 1962 occasion was the noted missionary-statesman, Dr. Walter Judd. Everyone there was impressed with his thoughtful and dynamic remarks on the subject, "The Christian College and Free Society." Among those impressed enough to do something about it besides applaud the speaker were Frank R. Seaver and M. Norvel Young, who agreed on the spot that the message needed to be distributed to a wider audience. Frank promptly offered to pay the cost if Pepperdine would print and distribute the speech. As always, he was as good as his word and soon several thousand copies of the message were circulated to influential people throughout the country.

In succeeding years, Mr. Seaver and the Seaver Institute which he headed made several more significant contributions to Ppperdine's National Citizenship program. When Frank Roger Seaver, who always planned with care and purpose, named the beneficiaries of his Last Will and Testament, Pepperdine College was among them.

Upon his death and in harmony with the direction his interest had taken, Blanche Ebert Seaver became an important and integral part of Pepperdine College and had a great influence on its growth to university status with its several campuses. Both Mrs. Seaver and Richard Seaver became members of the University Board of Pepperdine. She was named "Outstanding Friend of Pepperdine for 1968." She was awarded the honorary Doctorate of Fine Arts degree in April, 1969. She was named to the Board of Regents in 1976. She made the greatest pace-setting gift — $1,350,000 — when it was announced that Pepperdine had received a gift of land in beautiful Malibu and was going to build a second campus there. She has multiplied that gift many times since with a commitment which may very well be one of the greatest donations ever made to private education.

"I believe," she says simply, "that Pepperdine University is doing the things that Frank would want me to support."

Mrs. Frank Roger Seaver

At the dedication of the General Douglas MacArthur Building at Valley Forge, built by Mrs. Seaver in honor of MacArthur and in memory of her husband who admired MacArthur deeply. At left of the monument is Mrs. Jean MacArthur, widow of General MacArthur, talking with Mr. Bo Callaway. Behind the marker, Colonel Bunker and General Johnson, long time associates of MacArthur. To right of marker are Mrs. Seaver, Richard Seaver, Ken Wells (one of founders of Freedoms Foundation), Dr. William S. Banowsky (speaker for the occasion), and Dr. M. Norvel Young.

Above, Mr. Richard Scaife of Pittsburgh, member of Pepperdine Board of Regents and major force in founding the Malibu campus, joins Mrs. Seaver in setting off charge for beginning of construction. At right, Mrs. Seaver is seen with architect and well known planner, William Pereira, who did major conceptual planning of the campus layout and construction theme of Mediterranean style.

Above: The science center complex typifies the dramatic architectural style of all the Seaver College structures. Below: Mid-day sun illuminates the fountain on the central plaza. The Los Angeles *Times* called the setting in Malibu "one of the most beautiful in all of higher education."

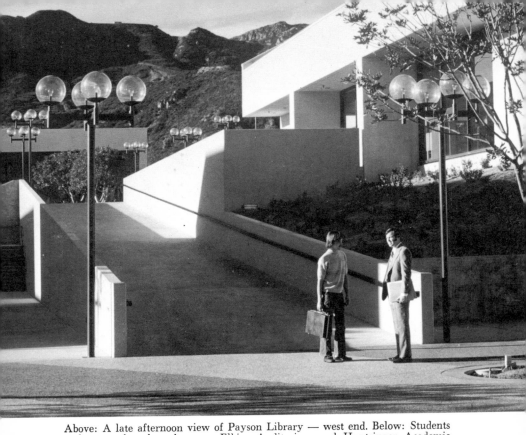

Above: A late afternoon view of Payson Library — west end. Below: Students gather on the plaza between Elkins Auditorium and Huntsinger Academic Complex during a class break.

Mrs. Blanche Seaver and Dr. William S. Banowsky, President of Pepperdine University at Century Plaza Hotel on the occasion of formal announcement of plans to build a new campus at Malibu. At right they are in Joslyn Plaza with Huntsinger Academic Complex in background, and the Brock House, home of the president, on the hill in distance.

At left, Mrs. Pepperdine (right) receives Seaver College into the family of schools of Pepperdine University, and gives Mrs. Seaver a copy of biography of her husband, "Faith Is My Fortune." Lower left, Richard Seaver at dedication of Seaver College. Right, Mrs. Seaver is joined on campus by Senator John Murphy, Nancy Reagan, Governor Ronald Reagan, and Chancellor M. Norvel Young.

At right, Mrs. Seaver is flanked by Governor Reagan, President Banowsky at dedication of Seaver College. Below, left, two sons of Richard Seaver, Carlton and Patrick, join Aunt Blanche. At right, Mrs. Seaver speaks about her husband at the dedication of the College honoring his name.

# 18

## "Not Here Long to Linger"

God called Frank Roger Seaver from this world to his eternal reward on October 31, 1964, when he was in his eighty-first year.

Blanche was summoned that morning to the hospital, where he had been confined a week following surgery. Doctors knew the end was near. He rallied briefly as she kissed him, recognized her and whispered an endearment. Then the great spirit of this man left his body as his beloved Blanche cradled his head in her arms.

On November 2, 1964, funeral services were conducted in the packed auditorium of the First Congregational Church where Frank had worshipped so long and faithfully over the years. It was one of the largest crowds ever assembled in the auditorium. Many of those wishing to attend could not get inside. The procession of members of all the boards on which Frank served was led by Henry Salvatori, his devoted friend. Appropriately, the man who said the great words of praise for the departed one and gave profound words of comfort for those left behind was Dr. James W. Fifield, Jr., beloved minister at First Congregational for many years and a close personal friend of Frank Seaver.

Fifield spoke as one Christian gentleman about another, with great love and admiration.

"Frank R. Seaver has entered into the larger life

which awaits us all. And we're gathered here in amazing numbers — by our presence to pay the tribute of our respect and our affection to his memory.

"The service is relatively simple. He wanted it so. We're not here long to linger, and we're not here to shed the tears for those who had not faith, because we have faith as he did.

"Those who knew him respected him. As they knew him better, they trusted him, and when they knew him well, loved him.

"The story of his life is well known to such as would gather for this service. It's an Horatio Alger story, with spiritual additions, and with an extraordinary impulse to do good which dominated all his years.

"There's a flag on his casket. He had patriotic devotions which put its lack in most of us to shame. He lost no opportunity to respond to the call of his country, and this was a characteristic of Frank Seaver from his enlistment until his last breath. No one came to him with any need on the part of his country and found a deaf ear. It is the general conviction of those who knew him best that he did more than his share in respect to all patriotic opportunities, to serve the country whose Flag is on his casket.

"He was an engineer. He approached his problems and their solutions in the frame of reference of an engineer, with thorough-going interest in details. He approached his personal responsibilities and interests as an engineer. Nothing was 'happenstantial' — everything was carefully thought out and finally decreed.

"He was a religious man, brought up in a fine Christian home, which happened to be Congregational. He spoke with great depth of affection and appreciation of the religious influence which his parents had provided in his life."

Dr. Fifield concluded his remarks,

"In my more than forty years' ministry, I have never discussed immortality with any man who was more intelligent about it or more deeply convinced of its validity than Frank Seaver. When I returned from a trip after interviewing thirty of the outer space scientists in connection with the spiritual hypothesis of life, commencing with an evening with Dr. Wernher von Braun and others, I talked with Mr. Seaver about it. Science is only beginning to understand the meaning of infinity and eternity. The metaphysical limitations are just being broken. David, when he sang his Psalms, understood the limitless power of an eternal God in ways modern science has not yet embraced. Mr. Seaver had the eternal perspective which is within the reach of us all in this era of outer space in ways never available to any other era in all human history. We would do well to emulate his perspective, which was eternal!"

Dr. Fifield concluded his remarks with a prayer and the hundreds of friends of Frank Roger Seaver silently filed out of the chapel. All were aware that his legacy would last.

# 19

## A Precious Partnership

It was September 15, 1966. The big United Air Lines jet roared onto the runway at O'Hare Field and Blanche Seaver said a silent prayer for a safe trip from Los Angeles.

Every time she flew she thought of Frank and the first air trip they made together. It had been to Hawaii, only six years earlier, and the only reason she had given in to going by air was that they were unable to make reservations on a ship.

"Even after the plane got into the air out over the Pacific," nephew Richard Seaver laughed afterward, "I kept expecting to see a parachute open and Aunt Blanche come floating down!"

Now she was landing in Chicago on the same airline she had been introduced to by Frank six years before. The big jet coasted flawlessly down the runway, braking, engines reversing, slowing to a halt at the disembarking area. Blanche and her traveling companions, sister Mabel and brother-in-law Lee Marks, had gathered up their belongings.

September 15 was Blanche Seaver's birthday. She was now in the city of her birth. But it was not her natal anniversary that had brought her to the Windy City. She had come back to be closer to and intimately remember what to her was the most important date in her life, September 16, 1916. For on the morrow she would observe the Golden Anniversary of her marriage to Frank Roger

Seaver. And her beloved would not be there, except in spirit, a very powerful and real force in her life.

That night they stayed in Evanston and Blanche made plans for the next day, a Friday. Memories flooded over her as she telephoned the church, North Shore Congregational, at Sheridan Road and Wilson. She remembered that the beautiful old edifice had been located in an exclusive area of homes fifty years ago when she and Frank had said their nuptial vows. She knew that now the neighborhood had deteriorated, as so many residential areas in so many American cities had during that period of time. She knew that the church where she and Frank were wed was now a haven for youngsters of the street. She knew, too, that the kindly minister who had united them had long ago gone to his reward.

"Reverend Kramer," the man's voice at the other end of the line identified himself.

It was a pleasant voice, young and warm. It invited confidence. Blanche Seaver, her heart pounding with the emotion of the moment, confided what was in her heart.

"I just want to sit and recall all I can of that glorious night," she concluded.

"Of course," the young minister agreed. "We'll do all we can to make it meaningful for you."

He hesitated, then said: "There's only one thing. Tomorrow night we'll have a group of youngsters in the recreation room. We might have a little noise from bouncing balls."

His voice trailed off, "maybe we could call off the games . . ."

Blanche thought of her husband's love of the young and smiled. He'd never object to a few bouncing balls! She assured Reverend Kramer this made not the slightest difference.

"Would you like for us to have some music?" the minister asked. "We have a very wonderful organist and I'm sure she would be delighted to play some of your favorite songs."

Blanche, whose own life has always been closely woven around music, liked the idea very much.

"Then we'll meet you at the steps with open arms," the minister assured.

The next evening some thirty other relatives of the Chicago area joined them for dinner and drove to the church. It was eight o'clock and, as they approached the beautiful old place of worship, the faint sounds of children's cries and the thud of a bouncing ball could be heard somewhere else in the building. Reverend Kramer, as he had promised, met them at the door and ushered them into seats close to the altar.

Tears came as Blanche looked upon that hallowed scene where she had promised exactly fifty years ago to "love, honor and obey . . ."

The soothing tones of the organ — softly and with painful loveliness — played the memorable music, "I Love You Truly," "Beloved It Is Morn," "Because . . ." And Blanche remembered with such clarity.

With the phrase "because God made you mine," Blanche, as an accomplished pianist and noted composer, knew she had never heard more beautiful and inspiring notes. Frank was at her side like that day so long ago . . . so near now . . . so fleeting that fifty years . . . She relaxed and let her memory sweeten her consciousness of this moving hour . . .

Later the young minister, so understanding and himself moved by the occasion, came to her quietly.

"Would you like for me to go up in the pulpit and read from the Bible?" he whispered gently.

"Yes," she whispered. "Yes, please do."

He read words of comfort from this Holy Book of Life

which further moved them all, the living, in this room. He read and he talked with earnest feeling on the subject of love. Nothing could have been more fitting, for surely this had been a romance made in heaven, and nothing of the love had waned even though one was now departed.

For Blanche Seaver — surrounded by people whose own lives had also been touched in very real ways over the years by this great man — it was a time of remembering, a time of faith, a time of renewing her vows of half a century ago to Frank Roger Seaver. Her promise now could only be to continue to devote her life totally to the things he held dear in his own long lifetime. She said so as bravely as she'd said "I do" fifty years ago.

On April 20, 1975, Seaver College of Pepperdine University was established as a monument to this precious partnership.

Because of his leadership in the founding of Seaver College, Dr. William S. Banowsky was able at the dedication of the College to focus on the essence of this partnership between Blanche and Frank Seaver. "Some lives," he said, "can best be characterized by biographical details, but Blanche Seaver's is not one of those. The biography is, of course, impressive. But knowing these facts about an important public figure is not the same as knowing Blanche. One of the private stories I know is that long ago, as a little girl, Blanche was allowed to assist in her father's paint and supply store. What she relished most was tailor cutting the pieces of glass which were ordered by her father's customers. What she is proudest of is that she never broke even one piece of glass. She was so dependable that she got to use her father's diamond-point glass cutter. 'Bill,' she recently said to me, 'please don't let them call me a philanthropist! I just feel like a little glass cutter.' It is Blanche Seaver's essential purity of heart, not these external credentials, which makes her character worthy of emulation. She embodies qualities of spirit and mind to which we hope young people in this college will always be pointed. Given the circumstances of wealth and ceremony which have surrounded her life, it is a tribute to her that she has remained such a natural, unaffected person."

And Dr. Banowsky added: "Mrs. Seaver has a tremendous capacity for love, a great appreciation of beauty. She is capable of natural joy. She is devoted to the standards of dignity and decency which are the finest tradition of Western civilization. She is a tireless worker with a voracious zest for life, and she is a person of transparent sincerity. As we all know, Blanche is not a shrinking violet who leaves us in doubt about her convictions. What is most important, she has the courage of her convictions. She not only stands up and speaks out when it is popular to do so, but is just as militant when she is a minority of one. Long ago she adopted for her life the stirring motto of Father James Keller: 'What *one* person can do!'

"Governor Reagan, our distinguished speaker today, will forgive me if I share with you a story known only to him and Blanche and me. On a Sunday afternoon in the winter of 1972, I took Blanche to the Governor's Pacific Palisades residence to get his help. For reasons of conscience, Blanche had chosen for the first time in her life to bolt the political party she and Mr. Seaver had encouraged for decades. Although most of her life-long friends were doing so, she was absolutely refusing to serve as an honorary delegate to the National Convention. My only concern was that it could eventually prove awkward to her to isolate herself in this way, but I had failed to make any headway whatsoever. Accordingly, I sought reinforcement from Governor Reagan. I can only say that after two hours of very persuasive arguments, Blanche replied to the Governor: 'Ron, I know I may be the only one who feels this way, but I must live with my conscience.' When the slate of honorary delegates, including most of the distinguished Republican leaders in California was drawn, Blanche Seaver's name was conspicuous by its absence. In retrospect, her conscientious stand seems not an embarrassment, but a compliment. And she had stood up against a couple of pretty persuasive guys that she likes a lot.

"I should add a special word about her capacity for loyalty. So fierce is her loyalty that Richard Seaver once observed wryly, 'Aunt Blanche's enemies may have no virtues, but her friends have no vices.' Her great patriotism is really a product of her deep loyalty. So is her continuing devotion to Frank Seaver. He died in October, 1964. For more than a decade, Mrs. Seaver has executed her work in his name and every Sunday afternoon, week after week and year after year, she has visited his grave in Forest Lawn.

"Underlying all of these qualities is a fundamental spirituality. Leaders of religion — Dr. James W. Fifield, Rabbi Magnin, Cardinal McIntyre — are the intimate friends at the center of her life. An incredibly non-materialistic philosophy of life has been the basis of her generosity. She knows that life does not consist in the abundance of possessions. She not only has neither a cottage in Carmel nor a home in Palm Springs, but she and Mr. Seaver have never even owned their family residence. She still rents the mellow old house at 20 Chester Place. She wears no jewelry, neglects her wardrobe, appears for the annual banquets year after year in the same familiar gowns.

"Her joy is not in getting but in giving, and I have never met a person who gets more joy out of giving. Not just big buildings but a bouquet of roses for a wedding anniversary, a candygram at Christmastime, Vitamin C tablets to her friends with the sniffles, a bottle of wheat germ for those who look anemic — always, the simple contagious joy of giving and giving and giving again.

"It has taken great faith and boldness to give away

many millions. We can name others who have been as materially blessed, but most people are more materialistic than Blanche. They lack the courage to give away those material things which define their very security. It is enormously inspiring to me that Blanche Seaver has never defined her security in material terms, and for that reason, she is profoundly secure.

"Mrs. Seaver clearly knows the difference between this brick and mortar and the soul of the college."

Hopefully, the thousands of students who will go forth from the brick and mortar buildings at Malibu in the decades to come, will find the true soul of the endeavor by giving of themselves, and in that, will reflect the spirit of purpose which is Seaver College and which is the true legacy of Frank R. Seaver.